The Revised
GRAIL PSALMS

The Revised
GRAIL PSALMS
a Liturgical psalter

Prepared by
the Benedictine Monks of Conception Abbey

With a Foreword by
Francis Cardinal George, O.M. I.

With an Introduction by
Abbot Gregory J. Polan, O.S.B.

GIA Publications, Inc.

The Revised Grail Psalms

G-7882
ISBN: 978-1-57999-837-0

Copyright © 2010 Conception Abbey/The Grail.
Exclusive worldwide agent: GIA Publications, Inc.,
7404 S. Mason Ave., Chicago, IL 60638, USA.
www.giamusic.com/rgp.

For reprint information, visit www.giamusic.com/rgp

Printed in the United States of America

CONGREGATION FOR DIVINE WORSHIP
AND THE DISCIPLINE OF THE SACRAMENTS

Prot. n. 172/09/L

UNITED STATES OF AMERICA

At the request of His Eminence Cardinal Francis Eugene George, Archbishop of Chicago, President of the Conference of Bishops of the United States of America, in a letter dated January 28, 2009, by virtue of the faculty given to this Congregation by the Supreme Pontiff BENEDICT XVI, we gladly approve and confirm the text of the English-language liturgical Psalter, as it appears in the appended copy, to be used in all future liturgical books.

In printed editions, mention must be made of the *recognitio* granted by this Congregation. Moreover, two copies of the printed text should be forwarded to this Congregation.

All things to the contrary notwithstanding.

From the offices of the Congregation for Divine Worship and the Discipline of the Sacraments, March 19, 2010.

✠ Antonio Card. Cañizares Llovera
Prefect

✠ Joseph Augustine Di Noia, OP
Archbishop-Secretary

FOREWORD

Francis Cardinal George, OMI
Archbishop of Chicago
President, United States Conference of
Catholic Bishops, 2007–2010

On December 4, 1963, the Second Vatican Council issued the *Constitution on the Sacred Liturgy (Sacrosanctum Concilium)*. In no. 24, the Liturgy Constitution reminds us of the paramount importance of Scripture in the celebration of the liturgy and the need "to promote that warm and living love for Scripture to which the venerable tradition of both Eastern and Western Rites gives testimony."

With the introduction of the vernacular, the need arose for a faithful and singable translation of the Psalms that could be used as the faithful's response to the proclamation of the word of God. One of the early texts embraced by the Church for use in the sacred liturgy was the 1963 edition of The Grail Psalms, which relied on the translation of the Psalms into French in *La Bible de Jérusalem* (1953). Father Joseph Gelineau's original work, which set these French texts to chant tones, became the basis for the English version of the Psalms produced in Great Britain by the Ladies of the Grail, a secular religious institute.

While the 1963 Grail Psalter had many virtues, it also had some weaknesses. First, it did not have access to the Latin critical text of Scripture commissioned by Pope Paul VI and known as the *Nova Vulgata*, which was published in 1979. Second, it sometimes sacrificed accuracy of translation in order to accommodate the musical settings, at times becoming more of a paraphrase than a literal translation. Third, the translation failed at times to preserve the rich imagery and beauty of the Hebrew Scriptures.

As a result of these weaknesses, a revision of the 1963 Psalter became necessary. Furthermore, various sung versions of the psalms that were more paraphrases than faithful translations had been introduced into the liturgy by bishops' conferences in several English-speaking nations to replace the texts of the psalms found in the Lectionary. This situation led the United States Conference of Catholic Bishops to propose a thorough revision of the 1963 Grail Psalter that would be based on both the original Hebrew text and the *Nova Vulgata*, and would also be in harmony with the norms of translation found in *Liturgiam Authenticam* (2001).

The revised translation of The Grail Psalms presented now to the Church is more accurate, poetic, and singable. I am confident that communities and individuals will benefit from incorporating these psalms into their daily and liturgical prayer. The Psalms are truly the Church's prayer book, which Jesus himself prayed during his life on earth. Hence, they ought to be an integral part of every Catholic's prayer life.

The Second Vatican Council's *Dogmatic Constitution on Divine Revelation (Dei Verbum)*, explained the value of reading and praying the Old Testament:

> Now the books of the Old Testament, in accordance with the state of mankind before the time of salvation established by Christ, reveal to all men the knowledge of God and of man and the ways in which God, just and merciful, deals with men. . . . These same books, then, give expression to a lively sense of God, sound wisdom about human life, and a wonderful treasury of prayers, and in them the mystery of our salvation is present in a hidden way. Christians should receive them with reverence. (no. 15)

The "wonderful treasury of prayers" mentioned above refers to the Psalms, the Church's first prayer book. Pope John Paul II explains the efficacy of praying the Psalms by reminding us that

> in singing the Psalms, the Christian feels a sort of harmony between the Spirit present in the Scriptures and the Spirit who dwells within him

through the grace of Baptism. More than praying in his own words, he echoes those 'sighs too deep for words' mentioned by St. Paul (cf. Rom. 8:26), with which the Lord's Spirit urges believers to join in Jesus' characteristic invocation: 'Abba! Father!' (Rom. 8:15; Gal. 4:6). (General Audience, April 4, 2001)

In his excellent book *The Spirit of the Liturgy*, Pope Benedict XVI says that among the various witnesses throughout Scripture to the singing of individuals and communities in the praise of God, the Book of Psalms becomes the proper source for understanding the importance of sung prayer in Christian worship. As our Holy Father says: "In their prayed poetry, the Psalms display the whole range of human experiences, which become prayer and song in the presence of God." He then goes on to say: "Quite spontaneously, the Psalter becomes the prayer book of the infant Church, which, with equal spontaneity, has become a Church that sings her prayers" (p. 139).

The Psalms are meant to be sung. The *General Instruction on the Liturgy of the Hours* makes this same point when it states:

> The Psalms are not readings nor were they specifically composed as prayers, but as poems of praise. Though sometimes they may be proclaimed like a reading, nevertheless, because of their literary character, they are rightly called in Hebrew *tehillim*, that is, "songs of praise," and in Greek *psalmoi*, "songs to be sung to the sound of the harp." In all the Psalms there is a certain musical quality that determines the correct way of praying them. Therefore, though a psalm may be recited without being sung even by an individual in silence, its musical character should not be overlooked. (no. 103)

At his General Audience on Wednesday, March 28, 2001, Pope John Paul II gave an extended catechesis on the use of the Psalms in Christian prayer, especially in the Liturgy of the Hours, which he recommended that all Catholics pray. In fact, Pope John Paul II calls the Psalter the "ideal source of Christian prayer." He then goes on to give various approaches to understanding the Psalms. As the pope says:

> The first would consist in presenting their literary structure, their authors, their formation, the contexts in which they were composed. It would also be fruitful to read them in a way that emphasizes their poetic character, which sometimes reaches the highest levels of lyrical insight and symbolic expression. It would be no less interesting to go over the Psalms and consider the various sentiments of the human heart expressed in them: joy, gratitude, thanksgiving, love, tenderness, enthusiasm, but also intense suffering, complaint, pleas for help and for justice, which sometimes lead to anger and imprecation. In the Psalms, the human being fully discovers himself. (no. 2)

While these approaches to understanding the Psalms have great value, the one approach that Pope John Paul II recommended above all was the way the religious meaning of the Psalms can be used in the prayer of Jesus' disciples to understand the mystery of Christ himself. As Pope John Paul II states: "The Fathers were firmly convinced that the Psalms speak of Christ. The risen Jesus, in fact, applied the Psalms to himself when he said to the disciples: "Everything written about me in the Law of Moses and the prophets and the psalms must be fulfilled" (Lk 24:44). The Fathers add that in the Psalms Christ is spoken to or it is even Christ who speaks. In saying this, they were thinking not only of the individual person of Christ, but of the *Christus totus*, the total Christ, composed of Christ the Head and his members."

Since the early Christians found the mystery of Christ revealed in the Psalms, it is no surprise that they chose them to be an integral part of the celebration of the Eucharist and the Liturgy of the Hours. This Christological interpretation of the Psalms is undoubtedly an important way to release the full potential of these beautiful prayers. Yet, the Church is also open to supplementing these prayers with hymns and canticles, which are part of our Christian heritage.

Therefore, let me share with you the conclusion to Pope John Paul II's inspiring catechesis on the Psalms:

> By praying the Psalms as a community, the Christian mind remembered and understood that it is impossible to turn to the Father who dwells in heaven without an authentic communion of life with one's brothers and sisters who live on earth. Moreover, by being vitally immersed in the Hebrew traditions of prayer, Christians learned to pray by recounting the *magnalia Dei*, that is, the great marvels worked by God both in the creation of the world and humanity, and in the history of Israel and the Church. This form of prayer drawn from Scripture does not exclude certain freer expressions, which will continue not only to characterize personal prayer, but also to enrich liturgical prayer itself, for example, with hymns and troparia. But *the Book of Psalms remains the ideal source of Christian prayer and will continue to inspire the Church in the new millennium.* (no. 5, italics added)

This new translation of the Psalter by the Benedictine Monks of Conception Abbey will provide the text for our sung prayer for years to come. It is a labor of love on their part and a gift to be cherished by us.

INTRODUCTION TO THE REVISED GRAIL PSALMS

Abbot Gregory J. Polan, OSB
Conception Abbey

The Songs of Israel—The Songs of the Church

In the late 1940s, Father Patrick Cummins, OSB, a monk of Conception Abbey and a scholar and translator of Scripture in his own right, wrote the following definition in the introduction to his own unpublished translation of the Book of Psalms:

> What is a psalm? Is it a prayer? A rhythmic prayer? A hymn? An oriental hymn? A Semitic hymn? A Hebrew hymn? The answer to all these questions is an ascending Yes. Hence, if we look at human literature as an ascending pyramid, then that pyramid is crowned by the Psalter. Man is most godlike when he sings to God. And among those who sing to God the Hebrew psalmist stands highest. In universality of sentiment, in keenness of conception, in rhythm of speech, in beauty of imagery, the Hebrew singer has no rivals.

The 150 Psalms have been the prayer book of both Jews and Christians from their beginnings as peoples of faith and worship. We can surely affirm that Jesus himself used and prayed the Psalms during his mortal life—in synagogue or temple worship, at home, and in his own personal prayer. The old adage *Lex orandi, lex credendi* (the way of prayer is the way of belief) suggests how significant these 150 prayers have been in the formation of communities of believers. The Book of Psalms has provided words to bring meaning to people's search for God in all of life's circumstances: in fear or joy, struggle or hope, pain or praise, despair or thanksgiving. Though some of these texts have been in use for more than two millennia, the prayers of the Psalter still retain a freshness that enables them to speak with poignancy to each succeeding generation, drawing those who read them into the quest for the deepest purpose of human life: to abide in the presence of their God.

How often in this quest do we find ourselves struggling to find words to express the manifold movements of the human heart! The Psalms provide a way into that unique chamber of the heart where one stands most free and open before God. Often, to our initial surprise, we find ourselves thinking, "The words of the Psalms express my inmost thoughts and feelings better than I could myself. These words say what I am trying to say to God." The character of the Psalms is universal and classic, touching the human heart and giving voice to the most intimate motions of our souls before the One who is both transcendent and immanent, incomprehensible yet alarmingly close. The Psalms take us from the heights of praise to the depths of distress with language that always gives rise to a life-giving hope. They are inspired!

Rightly have the Psalms been called "a school of prayer." As these prayers give voice to so many of the experiences presented in the stories of the Bible, they come to us as words that have already been cried, shouted, and sung by people of faith throughout the centuries. Facing the human struggles of illness, imminent death, bigger-than-life enemies, and warring nations, the psalmist gave expression to the fears and uncertainties that troubled the present situation. Similarly, the joy of victory, the gratitude for prayers answered, and wonder at the marvels of creation all become part of the praise that is lifted up to the God who rules the world and brings all life into being. The psalmist attests with unshakable conviction that the One and Almighty God who touches every movement of history and each human life is the focus of all praise, the healer of every ill, and the source of all blessing.

The Psalms, then, are the prayer book of the Bible. They express responses appropriate to every situation found on the pages of Sacred Scripture. One need merely look at the lectionary of the Church—or of the Synagogue, for that matter—to see this. In Christian congregations, after hearing and reflecting on the word of God proclaimed in the readings, we answer with the singing of a psalm: our response to the voice of God we have heard speaking to the Church. The words of the psalm echo the words of the reading, and then lift the heart in prayer. As God has spoken to the assembled congregation in the sacred word, so the people, through the psalm, respond to God. Such dialogue lies at the heart of each individual's relationship with God. The Psalms have been an instrument of that dialogue for as long as they have been prayed by people of faith.

To the superlative status of the Psalms as the pinnacle of human literary expression, we may add the observation that the different genres or literary forms found in them give expression to both the wide-ranging life situations and the varying moods of the person of faith before God. The *hymn* lifts up praise to the God who has created the world and all its wonders. The *lament* brings before God the pain of alienation from God and neighbor, the struggle with doubts and fears, the anger that rises from disgrace and mistreatment, the fear of threatening illness and approaching death, the anguish of personal loss and a community's demise. The *thanksgiving* reminds the community that gratitude must be given to God who hears and answers those in need. The *wisdom* psalms reflect the insight and spiritual understanding that leads to a life lived with faith, hope, and love.

At the beginning of many psalms, unfamiliar expressions like "A *mitzmor* of David, with instrumental music, on the *gittith*," may sometimes be found. The names of Korah (Psalms 42, 44–49) and Asaph (Psalm 50, 73–83), frequently attached to such expressions, identify two of the musical guilds of the Jerusalem Temple, where the Psalms were originally prayed. Many of these phrases tell us that the Psalms were intended to be sung, often with specified accompaniment. The Hebrew title for the Book of Psalms is *Sepher Tehillim*, which translates "A Book of Sung Praises," further indicating the manner in which these prayers were to be rendered. Music clothes and elevates a text. It holds a special power to express what often cannot be accomplished in spoken words alone. It gives added expression that not only enhances the meaning but lifts the words to the level of inspiring prayer. This truth provides yet another insight into the profound and inspiring message of the Psalms. They were created to be sung, so as to give the words a second soul.

As songs of the early Church, the Psalms were not merely prayer, however; they were prophecy as well. In Luke's account of the risen Christ appearing and speaking to his disciples in Jerusalem, the text reads, "[Jesus] said to them, 'These are my words that I spoke to you while I was still with you, that everything written about me in the law of Moses and in the prophets and psalms must be fulfilled.' Then he opened their minds to understand the scriptures" (Lk 24:44 NAB). The authors of the New Testament use the Psalms extensively to speak of the mystery of Christ as the Messiah, the Anointed One.[1] For them, the Psalms held a key to understanding Jesus as the long-awaited Messiah. And as the early Church began to develop its liturgical year, annually celebrating the life, suffering, death, and resurrection of Christ, the *messianic* psalms played a substantial role in unfolding that great mystery of faith.

In Praise of the 1963 Grail Psalms

Perhaps the most significant change to emerge from the Second Vatican Council, a change that touched the life of every worshiper in the Roman Catholic Church, was the restoration of the vernacular to the liturgy. For centuries, Catholics had been used to hearing the Mass and the Divine Office read and sung in Latin. As the faithful began to celebrate the Mass in English, the need arose for new and inspiring texts and chants that would engage and encourage the participation of worshipers.

One of the most successful of these new liturgical texts was *The Grail Psalms*. Introduced in England in 1963 by the Ladies of the Grail (a secular religious institute), these texts had originally been translated into English from the Psalms

---

[1] Several salient passages in which the New Testament authors quote the Psalms are: Mt 21:9//Mk11:9//Lk 19:38//Jn 12:13 quotes Ps 118:26; Mt 21:42//Mk 12:10–11//Lk 20:17 quotes Ps 118:22–23; Mt 22:44//Mk 12:36//Lk 20:42–43 quotes Ps 110:1; Mt 27:46 quotes Ps 22:2; Jn 19:24 quotes Ps 22:19; Jn 19:36 quotes Ps 34:19; Acts 2:34–35 quotes Ps 110:1; Acts 4:25–26 quotes Ps 2:1–2; Heb 1:5 quotes Ps 2:7; Heb 1:6 quotes Ps 97:7; Heb 1:7 quotes Ps 104:4 (LXX); Heb 1:8 quotes Ps 45:7–8; Heb 1:10–12 quotes Ps 102:26–28; Heb 1:13 quotes Ps 110:1; Heb 2:6–7 quotes Ps 8: 5–7.

of the French *Bible de Jérusalem*. Some of these had been effectively set to chant tones by Rev. Joseph Gelineau, SJ, who had collaborated on the revision of those texts for *La Bible de Jérusalem* in 1953. Father Gelineau had become interested in preparing French texts of the Psalms with reference to the ancient Hebrew rhythmic patterns—specifically for singing. His efforts had become known to Rev. Dom Albert Derzelle, OCSO, Prior of Caldey Abbey in Wales, who in turn made them familiar to the Ladies of the Grail, expressing the hope that Father Gelineau's success might be reproduced in an English version of the Psalms. The Grail assembled a team consisting of two Hebrew scholars, Rev. Gall Schuon, OCSO, of Scourmont Abbey (Chimay, Belgium) and Rev. Hubert Richards, priest of the Archdiocese of Westminster; musical and liturgical expert Rev. Dom Gregory Murray, OSB, of Downside Abbey; and Philippa Craig of The Grail, whose task was to be (in her own words) the "Englishing" of the translation. The resulting texts were an instant success; they proved remarkably sensitive to the requirements of choral recitation and chanting, were adaptable to the exigencies of different musical settings, and were expressed in words and phrases that were easy to comprehend. For priests, monks, nuns, and religious, whose lives included the daily celebration of Mass and the Liturgy of the Hours (usually referred to as the Divine Office in former times), such a translation of the Psalms in English was essential for a smooth transition to the new forms of the liturgy. Possessing all these qualities and more, the 1963 Grail Psalms became a primary vehicle for Christian prayer; over the years since, they have come to shape the worship and spiritual life of countless communities and individuals in the English-speaking world.

The liturgical renewal of the Second Vatican Council also encouraged people of every state in life—laity as well as priests and religious—to pray the Liturgy of the Hours. This was after all "the public prayer of the Church," a repository of great spiritual riches from which all the faithful might benefit. The 1963 Grail Psalms opened the door for many people to become more familiar with the language and imagery of the Bible in a way that was inviting, enriching, and satisfying. As one colleague in the field of Scripture studies asserted, "Over the years of their use, The Grail Psalms have become to Catholics what the King James Version of the Bible has been to Protestant Churches."

What are the qualities that distinguish the 1963 Grail Psalms? For many Catholics, who may have known little of the Bible in English, The Grail Psalms became an avenue into understanding and appreciating the whole of the Old Testament. Hearing of God, who was for his people both victorious warrior and gentle shepherd, the One who hears our single voice in prayer and who calls us to live faithfully— this made clear how intimate was the relationship each person shares with God. Simple expressions like "Be still and know that I am God" (Ps 46:11), "Create a pure heart in me, O God" (Ps 51:12), "Mercy and faithfulness have met, justice and peace have embraced" (Ps 85:11), "Friend and neighbor you have taken away; my one companion is darkness" (Ps 88:19), and "O Lord, you search me and you know me; you know my resting and my rising" (Ps 139:1– 2a)—all these expressions continue to resonate in the hearts of many, bespeaking their own prayer to God. Such phrases lend themselves to effortless recall, becoming the very fabric of our interior life.

The "sprung rhythm" in which The Grail Psalms were composed made them easy to recite in common (that is, in a group setting) and easy to sing as chant.[2] Setting aside the stricter expectations of more formal poetic conventions, this rhythmic style imitates regular speech patterns more closely. Sprung rhythm possesses in vocal use something both natural and beautiful, a quality of simplicity and regularity one finds in reading through the lines of a Grail psalm. The very ebb and flow of the lines make these psalms conducive to prayer and reflection. And importantly, these rhythmic patterns bear a notable similarity to those in which the Hebrew Psalms

---

[2] Sprung rhythm imitates natural speech patterns, designating a certain number of major accents per line, while having an unfixed number of unstressed syllables, with no more than four syllables between each foot. Gerard Manley Hopkins, the nineteenth-century British poet and Jesuit priest, is said to have coined the expression, calling it "the most natural of things" in spoken poetry. A series of psalm tones, based on the Gregorian and Ambrosian modes, were developed by Fr. Joseph Gelineau, SJ, allowing The Grail Psalms to be sung in a recitative manner that clothes the text inspiringly and respects their sprung rhythm.

were composed—a similarity that is still evident today when they are prayed aloud in the Synagogue.

The language used in the 1963 Grail Psalms was easily understood by the person in the pew; no background in scriptural theology was needed to understand the general import of the text. At the same time, its poetic quality and beauty also could inspire the sensitive reader to ponder on further levels these simple yet profound and noble expressions of faith. It gave those who prayed it a language steeped in the inspired word, language for petition, praise, thanksgiving, confidence, hope, courage, faith, sorrow, human struggle before God, and love of God, neighbor, and creation. It gave people a form for their own internal conversation with God.

Why a Revision of the 1963 Grail Psalms?

The excellent qualities of the 1963 Grail Psalms might give rise to the question "Why make a revision?" There are several compelling reasons. As with anything that has generated such positive appreciation, there are also negative criticisms to be made. While the rhythmic quality and consistency in The Grail Psalms merits praise, the sometimes strict adherence to these rhythmic patterns too frequently forced its translators to *paraphrase* the text rather than translate it literally. Our revision maintains the sprung rhythm while at the same time striving for a more authentic translation of many paraphrased lines, in keeping with the principles set forth in *Liturgiam Authenticam*, the document published in 2001 by the Congregation for Divine Worship and the Discipline of the Sacraments as a guide for the translation of liturgical texts. Those who have prayed the 1963 Grail Psalms for many years will find great similarities in this revision, but they will also encounter some very different expressions of language in the newly translated elements.

Furthermore, considerable strides have been made in biblical scholarship since the 1950s and early 1960s, when The Grail translations were produced. We have come to a better understanding of many of the rhetorical devices used by the Hebrew psalmists, and these insights have been incorporated into the revision. Our understanding of the literary genres and patterns of thought found in the Psalms has also developed greatly; this too enables us to translate these ancient texts with greater accuracy.

And while building on the good and inspiring elements of the first edition has the potential to provide continuity for those who have prayed The Grail Psalms during these past five decades, we must be cognizant of those who will use this Psalter in the future as the Church continues to renew her liturgy. For the rising generations who will celebrate the Mass and the Liturgy of the Hours, it is our genuine hope that this revision of The Grail Psalms will be an effective vehicle for prayer, contemplation, and interior renewal of heart. Even as it seeks to present more authentic renderings of the ancient texts, it also hopes to provide more inclusive forms of expression—forms that are often truer to the original Hebrew than were the 1963 Grail Psalms. We dare to hope that the movement of Divine Providence is discernible in the fact that this translation was presented to several national episcopal conferences for consideration as a Liturgical Psalter just as the 2008 Synod on the Word and Its Teaching and Mission for the Church completed its meetings and discussions. If this revision of the 1963 Grail Psalms helps to forward the renewal that the Synod was convened to address, it will have fulfilled its purpose.

What Is Distinctive about a Liturgical Psalter?
A Liturgical Psalter takes into consideration the way the Psalms have actually been used in the Church's liturgy through the centuries. While the Book of Psalms was originally written and prayed in Hebrew, it is important to remember that the early Christian Church's Bible, both Old and New Testaments, was in Greek. The New Testament authors who quoted the Old Testament did so from the Septuagint—the Greek Bible that was the first translation of the Hebrew Scriptures. In their reflection on the meaning of the Messiah, the Christ, they delineated in the Septuagint the unfolding of the meaning of this great mystery of faith. They read the Psalms as one part of the prophetic

word explaining the coming of Christ, his mission, his teaching, his life, death, and resurrection. These reflections and insights were incorporated into the liturgy and also taken into consideration as the texts of Scripture were later translated by St. Jerome into the Latin Vulgate.

A Liturgical Psalter considers these historical circumstances in its translation of the biblical texts. Thus the primary source of the translation remains the Hebrew Bible, the Masoretic Text, but at certain junctures, both the Greek Bible (the Septuagint) and the Latin Bible (the Vulgate) are considered as sources bearing on the translation. Following the Second Vatican Council, Pope Paul VI commissioned a group of Benedictine monks to prepare a Latin critical text of the Scriptures that would be used for the text of the *Missale Romanum*; this text is known as the *Nova Vulgata*, which has been consulted in the translation of *The Revised Grail Psalms*.

An example of this approach may be illustrative. The author of the Epistle to the Hebrews affirms the humanity and divinity of Jesus Christ by quoting Psalm 8:5, "What is man that you should keep him in mind, the son of man that you care for him?" In the original Hebrew setting of its composition, the psalm verse refers to the human person as the pinnacle of God's creation. But when this text is quoted in the liturgy as a reference to Christ (at Christmas, for example, when the Church celebrates the mystery of the Incarnation), it is important (after the example of the Epistle to the Hebrews) that the praying Church see and understand the psalm as a reference to Christ. Thus in this liturgical context the Septuagint is used for rendering the text.

The hope is that this method will provide greater continuity between the texts we hear proclaimed at the liturgy and the psalms we chant to enhance our interior reception of those texts. The variety of translations used in our liturgical celebrations has sometimes served to obscure the connection between the readings and the corresponding psalms. We hope that our attention to the ways the Psalter is translated for specific use in the liturgy will clarify this connection. It is important to note that, while the preparation of this text belongs to a few individuals, it remains ultimately a document of the whole Church, and thus is subject to the Church's judgment "in order to maintain the tradition of interpretation that is proper to the Latin Liturgy" (*Liturgiam Authenticam*, no. 24). The text of this revision has been carefully examined by the Congregation for Divine Worship and the Discipline of the Sacraments, who are the final redactors of this work.

We have retained in this edition the practice of indicating the accents of the sprung rhythm for recitation and chanting of the Psalms. It is our hope that these marked accents will facilitate a prayerful and inspiring chanting or reading of the Psalms for communities who pray the Liturgy of the Hours in common or for individuals who might wish to recite or chant them aloud.

A Word for Those Unfamiliar with the Book of Psalms

Every day, people are becoming acquainted with the Psalter for the first time. Some have told me that, when they first heard or read from the Book of Psalms as a child or adolescent, they did not understand it and never felt drawn back to it. Others are aware of the Psalms but simply have not read or prayed seriously with them. Yet interest in this biblical book of 150 prayers continues to grow.

One way to become acquainted with the Psalter is through seeking effective ways to express our human need for God. We find ourselves in different situations in life that compel us to communicate our situation to the Lord. As we come to realize that all blessing comes from God, we experience the need to lift up words of praise and thanks to God. In moments of sadness, disappointment, frustration, and even anger, the Almighty is the One to whom we turn in hope of a reversal of our present situation. Turning to the Psalter to give expression to our need before God is a good way to become familiar with the prayers that people of faith have used for centuries both in their private prayer and in liturgical celebrations.

Below is a short list of different circumstances that frequently lead a person to prayer. For each of these, we suggest corresponding psalms to give appropriate expression to these circumstances. We hope that this might facilitate for the newcomer to the Psalms the opening of new avenues of satisfying and enriching prayer. The list is not intended to be exhaustive but rather to present some of the best-known and most frequently used Psalms under familiar headings; some psalms are listed more than once.

1. A Morning Prayer—Psalms 3, 5, 63, 143
2. An Evening Prayer—Psalms 130, 141
3. A Night Prayer—Psalms 4, 91, 134
4. Praise of God—Psalms 8, 66, 104, 135, 136, 145, 148, 150
5. Thanksgiving to God—Psalms 30, 34, 92, 111, 116, 118, 138
6. Prayer for Upright Living—Psalms 1, 15, 24, 37, 112
7. Prayer for Forgiveness—Psalms 32, 51, 80, 86
8. Longing for Union with God—Psalms 12, 27, 42, 63, 139
9. The Vanity of Human Life—Psalm 39, 49, 73, 90
10. Laments to Life's Struggles—Psalms 22, 25, 31, 40, 90
11. Confidence in God—Psalms 4, 16, 23, 25, 46, 131, 139
12. Hymns about the Messiah—Psalms 2, 23, 45, 89, 110, 132
13. Prayer in Old Age—Psalms 71, 90, 139
14. Historical Psalms—Psalms 78, 105, 106, 135, 136
15. Prayer in Times of Danger—Psalms 7, 28, 35, 38, 54, 56, 140

The Liturgy of the Hours has been of particular significance in the Church's formal use of the Psalms as prayer. But the Church has always intended that the formal recitation of the Psalms be a source of inspiration for personal prayer as well. An integral element of the practice of *lectio divina*, the slow and reflective reading of Scripture, is to pray directly from the biblical text. We do this in the liturgy when, after the proclamation of Scripture and a short period for silent reflection, the congregation sings a responsorial psalm. The psalm serves as the prayer of the community, responding to the voice of God heard in the biblical reading, but we can certainly make use of the same method when we pray the Psalms by ourselves: reading the text of the psalm, reflecting on it, and then lifting up to God our own words that arise from our meditative encounter with the text.

Reading and praying in this manner—placing the texts of the Psalms at the heart of our prayer—we are formed in the spirit of the Bible's own prayer book. Whether in community liturgical prayer or in prayer of the heart alone in one's room, these ancient prayers of the Synagogue and the Church have taught generations of faith-filled people the way of redemption as it is lived out in everyday life. Their universal message continues to inspire people to open wide their hearts to a God whose word to us is "ever ancient, ever new" (St. Augustine). The Psalms become our daily companion in prayer and our daily conversation with the living God, who has created us for just that purpose.

Acknowledgments

When this work of the revision of the 1963 Grail Psalms was undertaken at the request of the United States Bishops' Committee on the Liturgy in 1998, we had no idea how extensive an effort would be required to bring it to a successful conclusion. The International Commission for the Preparation of an English Lectionary (established by the Bishops' Conferences of England and Wales, Scotland, Ireland, New Zealand, and Australia, with the approval of the Holy See) expressed interest in the adoption of *The Revised Grail Psalms* for use in their new lectionary, so members of that body were consulted extensively in the preparation of the final text; their biblical expertise brought theological richness, poetic beauty, and pastoral sensitivity to our rendering. The work of the monks of Conception Abbey involved in producing the work beyond translation included proofreading, musical considerations, and computer layout, as well as suggestions to improve felicity of expression in both grammar and syntax of both the text and ancillary documents. And finally, it is worth noting that the monks of Conception Abbey prayed *The Revised Grail Psalms* for several years before the text was finalized, engaging them with heart and soul, and offering suggestions for improvement and words of encouragement for what we hoped would eventually emerge as yet one more contribution from the Benedictine Order to the ongoing growth and development of the Church's liturgy.

BOOK ONE
Of The Psalter

Psalm 1

1 Blessed indeed is the man
   who follows not the counsel of the wicked,
   nor stands in the path with sinners,
   nor abides in the company of scorners,
2 but whose delight is the law of the LORD,
   and who ponders his law day and night.

3 He is like a tree that is planted
   beside the flowing waters,
   that yields its fruit in due season,
   and whose leaves shall never fade;
   and all that he does shall prosper.

4 Not so are the wicked, not so!
   For they, like winnowed chaff,
   shall be driven away by the wind.

5 When the wicked are judged they shall not rise,
   nor shall sinners in the council of the just;
6 for the LORD knows the way of the just,
   but the way of the wicked will perish.

Psalm 2

¹ Why do the nations conspire,
   and the peoples plot in vain?
² They arise, the kings of the earth;
   princes plot against the Lord and his Anointed.
³ "Let us burst asunder their fetters.
   Let us cast off from us their chains."

⁴ He who sits in the heavens laughs;
   the Lord derides and mocks them.
⁵ Then he will speak in his anger,
   his rage will strike them with terror.
⁶ "It is I who have appointed my king
   on Sion, my holy mountain."

⁷ I will announce the decree of the Lord:
   The Lord said to me, "You are my Son.
   It is I who have begotten you this day.

8 Ask of me and I will give you
   the nations as your inheritance,
   and the ends of the earth as your possession.
9 With a rod of iron you will rule them;
   like a potter's jar you will shatter them."

10 So now, O kings, understand;
   take warning, rulers of the earth.
11 Serve the LORD with fear;
   exult with trembling, pay him your homage,
12 lest he be angry and you perish on the way,
   for suddenly his anger will blaze.

Blessed are all who trust in God!

Psalm 3

¹ *A Psalm of David as he is fleeing from his son Absalom.*

² How many are my foes, O Lord!
How many are rising up against me!
³ How many are saying about me,
"There is no help for him in God."

⁴ But you, Lord, are a shield about me,
my glory, who lift up my head.
⁵ I cry aloud to the Lord.
From his holy mountain he answers me.

⁶ I lie down, I sleep and I wake,
for the Lord upholds me.
⁷ I will not fear even thousands of people
who are ranged on every side against me.

Arise, Lord; save me, my God,
⁸ you who strike all my foes on the cheek,
you who break the teeth of the wicked!
⁹ Salvation belongs to the Lord;
may your blessing be on your people!

Psalm 4

¹ *For the Choirmaster. With stringed instruments.*
   A Psalm of David.

² I called, the God of justice gave me answer;
   from anguish you released me, have mercy and
      hear me!

³ Children of man, how long will my glory be
      dishonored,
   will you love what is futile and seek what is false?

⁴ Know that the LORD works wonders for his
      faithful one;
   the LORD will hear me whenever I call him.

⁵ Tremble, do not sin: ponder on your bed and be
      still.
⁶ Offer right sacrifice, and trust in the LORD.

⁷ "What can bring us happiness?" many say.
   Lift up the light of your face on us, O LORD.

⁸ You have put into my heart a greater joy
   than abundance of grain and new wine can
      provide.

⁹ In peace I will lie down and fall asleep,
   for you alone, O LORD, make me dwell in safety.

Psalm 5

¹ *For the Choirmaster. With flutes. A Psalm of David.*

² To my words give ear, O LORD;
   give heed to my sighs.
³ Attend to the sound of my cry,
   my King and my God.

⁴ To you do I pray, O LORD.
   In the morning you hear my voice;
   in the morning I plead and watch before you.

⁵ You are no God who delights in evil;
   no sinner is your guest.
⁶ The boastful shall not stand their ground
   before your eyes.

⁷ All who do evil you despise;
   all who lie you destroy.
   The deceitful and those who shed blood,
   the LORD detests.

⁸ Yet through the greatness of your merciful love,
   I enter your house.
   I bow down before your holy temple,
   in awe of you.

⁹ Lead me, LORD, in your justice,
    because of my foes;
      make straight your way before me.

¹⁰ No truth can be found in their mouths,
    their heart is all malice,
      their throat a wide-open grave;
      with their tongue they flatter.

¹¹ Declare them guilty, O God.
    Let them fail in their designs.
      Drive them out for their many transgressions,
      for against you have they rebelled.

¹² All who take refuge in you shall be glad,
    and ever cry out their joy.
      You shelter them; in you they rejoice,
      those who love your name.
¹³ It is you who bless the just one, O LORD;
    you surround him with your favor like a shield.

Psalm 6

¹ *For the Choirmaster. With stringed instruments,*
   upon the Eighth Chord. A Psalm of David.

² O LORD, do not rebuke me in your anger;
   reprove me not in your rage.
³ Have mercy on me, LORD, for I languish.
   LORD, heal me; my bones are shaking,
⁴ and my soul is greatly shaken.

   But you, O LORD, how long?
⁵ Return, LORD, rescue my soul.
   Save me in your merciful love.
⁶ For in death there is no remembrance of you;
   from the grave, who can give you praise?

⁷ I am exhausted with my groaning;
   every night I drench my bed with tears,
   I bedew my couch with weeping.
⁸ My eyes waste away with grief;
   I have grown old surrounded by all my foes.

⁹ Leave me, all who do evil,
   for the LORD heeds the sound of my weeping.
¹⁰ The LORD has heard my plea;
   the LORD will receive my prayer.
¹¹ All my foes will be shamed and greatly shaken,
   suddenly put to shame.

Psalm 7

1 *A Lament of David that he chanted to the L*ORD *on account of Cush, the Benjaminite.*

2 O Lord, my God, I take refuge in you.
   Save and rescue me from all my pursuers,
3 lest they tear me apart like a lion,
   and drag me off with no one to rescue me.

4 If I have done this, O Lord, my God,
5 if I have paid back evil for good,
   I who saved my unjust oppressor:
6 then let my foe pursue my soul and seize me;
   let him trample my life to the ground,
   and lay my honor in the dust.

7 O Lord, rise up in your anger;
   be exalted against the fury of my foes.
   Awake, my God, to enact
   the justice you ordered.
8 Let the company of peoples gather round you,
   as you take your seat above them on high.

9 The Lord is judge of the peoples.
   Give judgment for me, O Lord,
   for I am just and blameless of heart.

¹⁰ Put an end to the evil of the wicked!
   Make the just man stand firm;
   it is you who test mind and heart,
   O God of justice!

¹¹ God is a shield before me,
   who saves the upright of heart.
¹² God is a judge, just and powerful and patient,
   not exercising anger every day.

¹³ Against someone who does not repent,
   God will sharpen his sword;
   he bends his bow and makes ready.
¹⁴ For such a one he prepares deadly weapons;
   he barbs his arrows with fire.

¹⁵ Here is one who conceives iniquity;
   pregnant with malice, he gives birth to lies.
¹⁶ He digs a pit and bores it deep;
   and in the trap he has made he falls.
¹⁷ His malice recoils on his head;
   on his own skull his violence falls.

¹⁸ I thank the LORD for his justice,
   singing to the name of the LORD, the Most High.

Psalm 8

¹ *For the Choirmaster. Upon the* gittith.
  A Psalm of David.

² O LORD, our Lord, how majestic
   is your name through all the earth!
   Your majesty is set above the heavens.
³ From the mouths of children and of babes
   you fashioned praise to foil your enemy,
   to silence the foe and the rebel.

⁴ When I see the heavens, the work of your fingers,
   the moon and the stars which you arranged,
⁵ what is man that you should keep him in mind,
   the son of man that you care for him?

⁶ Yet you have made him little lower than the angels;
   with glory and honor you crowned him,
⁷ gave him power over the works of your hands:
   you put all things under his feet,

⁸ All of them, sheep and oxen,
   yes, even the cattle of the fields,
⁹ birds of the air, and fish of the sea
   that make their way through the waters.
¹⁰ O LORD, our Lord, how majestic
   is your name through all the earth!

Psalm 9

¹ *For the Chorimaster. In the manner of a Chant*
   Mut Labben. *A Psalm of David.*

² I will praise you, Lord, with all my heart;
   all your wonders I will confess.
³ I will rejoice in you and be glad,
   and sing psalms to your name, O Most High.

⁴ See how my enemies turn back,
   how they stumble and perish before you.
⁵ You upheld the justice of my cause;
   you sat enthroned, an upright judge.

⁶ You have rebuked the nations, destroyed the wicked;
   you have wiped out their name forever and ever.
⁷ The foe is destroyed, eternally ruined.
   You uprooted their cities; their memory has perished.

⁸ But the Lord sits enthroned forever;
   he has set up his throne for judgment.
⁹ He will judge the world with justice;
   he will govern the peoples with equity.

¹⁰ For the oppressed, the Lord will be a stronghold,
   a stronghold in times of distress.
¹¹ Those who know your name will trust you;
   you will not forsake those who seek you, O Lord.

¹² Sing psalms to the LORD who dwells in Sion.
  Tell his mighty works among the peoples,
¹³ for the Avenger of Blood has remembered them,
  has not forgotten the cry of the poor.

¹⁴ Have mercy on me, O LORD;
  see how I suffer from my foes,
  you who raise me from the gates of death,
¹⁵ that I may recount all your praise
  at the gates of daughter Sion,
  and rejoice in your salvation.

¹⁶ The nations have fallen in the pit which they
      made;
  their feet have been caught in the snare they laid.
¹⁷ The LORD has revealed himself; he has given
      judgment.
  The wicked are snared by the work of their hands.

¹⁸ Let the wicked go down to the grave,
  all the nations forgetful of God:
¹⁹ for the needy shall not always be forgotten,
  nor the hopes of the poor ever perish.

²⁰ Arise, O LORD, let human strength not prevail!
  Let the nations be judged before you.
²¹ Strike them with terror, O LORD;
  let the nations know they are but men.

Psalm 10 *(9:22–39)*

¹ O Lᴏʀᴅ, why do you stand afar off,
  and hide yourself in times of distress?
² The poor are devoured by the pride of the wicked;
  they are caught in the schemes that others have
      made.

³ For the wicked boasts of his soul's desires;
  the covetous blasphemes and spurns the Lᴏʀᴅ.
⁴ The wicked says in his pride, "God will not
      punish.
  There is no God." Such are his thoughts.

⁵ His path is ever untroubled;
  your judgments are on high, far removed.
  All those who oppose him, he derides.
⁶ In his heart he thinks, "Never shall I falter;
  never shall misfortune be my lot."

⁷ His mouth is full of cursing, guile, oppression;
  under his tongue are deceit and evil.
⁸ He sits in ambush in the villages;
  in hidden places, he murders the innocent.

  The eyes of the wicked keep watch for the helpless.
⁹ He lurks in hiding like a lion in his lair;
  he lurks in hiding to seize the poor;
  he seizes the poor one and drags him away.

¹⁰ He crouches, preparing to spring,
   and the helpless fall prey to his strength.
¹¹ He says in his heart, "God forgets,
   he hides his face, never will he see."

¹² Arise, O Lord; lift up your hand, O God!
   Do not forget the poor!
¹³ Why should the wicked spurn God,
   saying in his heart, "You will not call to
        account"?

¹⁴ But you have seen the trouble and sorrow.
   You note it; you take it in your hands.
   The helpless one relies on you,
   for you are the helper of the orphan.

¹⁵ Break the arm of the wicked and the sinner!
   Pursue their wickedness till nothing remains!
¹⁶ The Lord is king forever and ever.
   The nations shall perish from his land.

¹⁷ O Lord, you have heard the desire of the poor.
   You strengthen their hearts; you turn your ear
¹⁸ to give right judgment for the orphan and
        oppressed,
   so that no one on earth may strike terror again.

Psalm 11 (10)

¹ For the Choirmaster. Of David.

In the LORD I have taken refuge.
How can you say to my soul,
"Fly like a bird to the mountain!

² Look, the wicked are bending their bow!
They are fixing their arrow on the string,
to shoot the upright of heart in the dark.
³ Foundations once destroyed,
what can the just man do?"

⁴ The LORD is in his holy temple;
the throne of the LORD is in heaven.
His eyes behold the world;
his gaze probes the children of men.

⁵ The LORD inspects the just and the wicked;
the lover of violence he hates.
⁶ He sends fire and brimstone on the wicked,
a scorching wind to fill their cup.
⁷ For the LORD is just and loves deeds of justice;
the upright shall behold his face.

Psalm 12 *(11)*

¹ *For the Choirmaster. Upon the Eighth Chord.*
   A Psalm of David.

² Save me, O Lord, for the holy ones are no more;
   the faithful have vanished from the sons of men.
³ They babble vanities, one to another,
   with cunning lips, with divided heart.

⁴ May the Lord destroy all cunning lips,
   the tongue that utters boastful words,
⁵ those who say, "We prevail with our tongue;
   our lips are our own, who is our master?"

⁶ "For the poor who are oppressed and the needy
         who groan,
   now will I arise," says the Lord;
   "I will grant them the salvation for which they
         long."
⁷ The words of the Lord are words without alloy,
   silver from the furnace, seven times refined.

⁸ It is you, O Lord, who will keep us safe,
   and protect us forever from this generation.
⁹ The wicked prowl on every side,
   while baseness is exalted by the sons of men.

Psalm 13 (12)

¹ For the Choirmaster. A Psalm of David.

² How long, O LORD? Will you forget me forever?
How long will you hide your face from me?
³ How long must I bear grief in my soul,
have sorrow in my heart all day long?
How long shall my enemy prevail over me?

⁴ Look, answer me, LORD my God!
Give light to my eyes lest I fall asleep in death;
⁵ lest my enemy say, "I have overcome him";
lest my foes rejoice when they see me fall.

⁶ As for me, I trust in your merciful love.
Let my heart rejoice in your salvation.
⁷ I will sing to the LORD who has been bountiful
with me.
I will sing psalms to the name of the LORD Most
High.

Psalm 14 (13)

¹ *For the Choirmaster. A Psalm of David.*

The fool has said in his heart,
"There is no God."
Their deeds are corrupt, depraved;
no one does any good.

² From heaven the LORD looks down
on the human race,
to see if any are wise,
if any seek God.

³ All have gone astray,
depraved, every one;
there is no one who does any good;
no, not even one.

⁴ Do none of the evildoers understand?
They eat up my people as if eating bread;
they never call out to the LORD.

⁵ There they shall tremble with fear,
for God is with the generation of the just.
⁶ You may mock the plans of one that is poor,
but his refuge is the LORD.

⁷ O that Israel's salvation might come from Sion.
When the LORD delivers his people from bondage,
then Jacob will be glad and Israel rejoice.

Psalm 15 (14)

¹ *A Psalm of David.*

LORD, who may abide in your tent,
and dwell on your holy mountain?
² Whoever walks without fault;
who does what is just,
and speaks the truth from his heart.

³ Whoever does not slander with his tongue,
who does no wrong to a neighbor,
who casts no slur on a friend,
⁴ who looks with scorn on the wicked,
but honors those who fear the LORD.

Who keeps an oath, whatever the cost,
⁵ who lends no money at interest,
and accepts no bribes against the innocent.
Such a one shall never be shaken.

Psalm 16 (15)

¹ *A Miktam. Of David.*

Preserve me, O God, for in you I take refuge.
² I say to the LORD, "You are my Lord.
My happiness lies in you alone."

³ As for the holy ones who dwell in the land,
   they are noble, and in them is all my delight.
⁴ Those who choose other gods increase their
           sorrows.
   I will not take part in their offerings of blood.
   Nor will I take their names upon my lips.

⁵ O LORD, it is you who are my portion and cup;
   you yourself who secure my lot.
⁶ Pleasant places are marked out for me:
   a pleasing heritage indeed is mine!

⁷ I will bless the LORD who gives me counsel,
   who even at night directs my heart.
⁸ I keep the LORD before me always;
   with him at my right hand, I shall not be moved.

⁹ And so, my heart rejoices, my soul is glad;
   even my flesh shall rest in hope.
¹⁰ For you will not abandon my soul to hell,
   nor let your holy one see corruption.

¹¹ You will show me the path of life,
   the fullness of joy in your presence,
   at your right hand, bliss forever.

Psalm 17 (16)

¹ *A Prayer of David.*

O L ORD, hear a cause that is just;
pay heed to my cry.
Turn your ear to my prayer:
no deceit is on my lips.
² From you may my justice come forth.
Your eyes discern what is upright.

³ Search my heart and visit me by night.
Test me by fire, and you will find no wrong in me.

⁴ My mouth does not transgress as others do;
on account of the words of your lips,
I closely watched the paths of the violent.

⁵ I kept my steps firmly in your paths.
My feet have never faltered.

⁶ To you I call; for you will surely heed me, O God.
Turn your ear to me; hear my words.
⁷ Display your merciful love.
By your right hand you deliver from their foes
those who put their trust in you.

⁸ Guard me as the apple of your eye.
 Hide me in the shadow of your wings
⁹ from the violent attack of the wicked.

 My foes encircle me with deadly intent.
¹⁰ Their hearts tight shut, their mouths speak
         proudly.
¹¹ They advance against me, and now they surround
         me.
 Their eyes watch to strike me to the ground.
¹² They are like a lion ready to claw,
 like some young lion crouched in hiding.

¹³ Arise, O Lᴏʀᴅ, confront them, strike them down!
 Let your sword deliver my soul from the wicked!
¹⁴ Let your hand, O Lᴏʀᴅ, deliver me from those
 whose portion in this present life is fleeting.

 May you give them their fill of your treasures;
 may their offspring rejoice in plenty,
 and leave their wealth to their children.
¹⁵ As for me, in justice I shall behold your face;
 when I awake I shall be filled with the vision of
         your presence.

Psalm 18 (17)

¹ *For the Choirmaster. Of David, the servant of the*
Lord, who spoke the words of this canticle to the
Lord when he had been freed from the power of
all his enemies and from the hand of Saul.
² *He said:*

I love you, Lord, my strength;
³ O Lord, my rock, my fortress, my savior;
my God, my rock where I take refuge;
my shield, my saving strength, my stronghold.
⁴ I cry out, "Praised be the Lord!"
and see, I am saved from my foes.

⁵ The waves of death rose about me;
the torrents of destruction assailed me;
⁶ the snares of the grave surrounded me;
the traps of death confronted me.

⁷ In my anguish I called to the Lord;
I cried to my God for help.
From his temple he heard my voice;
my cry to him reached his ears.

⁸ The earth then reeled and rocked;
the mountains were shaken to their base;
they quaked at his terrible anger.

⁹ Smoke came forth from his nostrils,
and scorching fire from his mouth;
from him were kindled live coals.

¹⁰ He bent the heavens and came down,
a black cloud was under his feet.
¹¹ On a cherub, he rode and he flew;
he soared on the wings of the wind.

¹² He made the darkness his covering,
the dark waters of the clouds, his tent.
¹³ A brightness shone out before him,
with hailstones and flashes of fire.

¹⁴ The LORD then thundered in the heavens;
the Most High let his voice be heard,
with hail and coals of fire.
¹⁵ He shot his arrows, scattered the foe,
flashed his lightnings, and put them to flight.

¹⁶ The bed of the ocean was revealed;
the foundations of the world were laid bare
at your rebuke, O LORD,
at the blast of the breath of your nostrils.

¹⁷ From on high he reached down and seized me;
he drew me forth from the mighty waters.
¹⁸ He saved me from my powerful foe,
from my enemies, whose strength I could not match.

¹⁹ They assailed me in the day of my misfortune,
  but the LORD was my strong support.
²⁰ He brought me out to a place of freedom;
  he saved me because he loved me.

²¹ The LORD rewarded me because I was just,
  repaid me, for my hands were clean,
²² for I have kept the ways of the LORD,
  and have not fallen away from my God.

²³ For his judgments are all before me;
  his commands I have not cast aside.
²⁴ I have been blameless before him;
  I have kept myself from guilt.
²⁵ The LORD repaid me because I was just,
  and my hands were clean in his eyes.

²⁶ With the faithful you show yourself faithful;
  with the blameless you show yourself blameless.
²⁷ With the sincere you show yourself sincere,
  but the cunning you outdo in shrewdness;
²⁸ for you save a lowly people,
  but bring low the eyes that are proud.

²⁹ It is you who give light to my lamp;
  the LORD my God lightens my darkness.
³⁰ With you I can break through a barrier,
  with my God I can scale a wall.

³¹ As for God, his way is blameless;
    the word of the LORD is pure.
    He indeed is the shield
    of all who trust in him.

³² For who is God but the LORD?
    Who is a rock but our God?
³³ It is God who girds me with strength,
    and keeps my path free of blame.

³⁴ My feet he makes swift as the deer's;
    he has made me stand firm on the heights.
³⁵ He has trained my hands for battle,
    and my arms to bend the bronze bow.

³⁶ You gave me your saving shield;
    with your right hand, you gave me support;
    you bent down to make me great.
³⁷ You lengthened my steps beneath me;
    and my feet have never slipped.

³⁸ I pursued and overtook my foes,
    never turning back till they were slain.
³⁹ I struck them so they could not rise;
    they fell beneath my feet.

⁴⁰ You girded me with strength for battle;
   you made my enemies fall beneath me.
⁴¹ You made my foes take flight;
   those who hated me I destroyed.

⁴² They cried out, but there was no one to save them,
   cried to the LORD, but he did not answer.
⁴³ I crushed them fine as dust before the wind,
   trod them down like dirt in the streets.

⁴⁴ From the feuds of the people you delivered me,
   and put me at the head of the nations.
   People unknown to me served me;
⁴⁵ when they heard of me, they obeyed me.

   Foreign nations came to me cringing;
⁴⁶ foreign nations faded away.
   Trembling, they came forth from their
         strongholds.

⁴⁷ The LORD lives, and blest be my Rock!
   May the God of my salvation be exalted,
⁴⁸ the God who gives me redress
   and subdues the peoples under me.

⁴⁹ You saved me from my furious foes;
   you set me above my assailants;
   you saved me from the violent man.
⁵⁰ So I will praise you, LORD, among the nations;
   to your name will I sing a psalm.

⁵¹ The LORD gives great victories to his king,
   and shows merciful love for his anointed,
   for David and his seed forever.

Psalm 19 (18)

[1] *For the Choirmaster. A Psalm of David.*

[2] The heavens declare the glory of God,
and the firmament proclaims the work of his hands.
[3] Day unto day conveys the message,
and night unto night imparts the knowledge.

[4] No speech, no word, whose voice goes unheeded;
[5] their sound goes forth through all the earth,
their message to the utmost bounds of the world.

[6] There he has placed a tent for the sun;
it comes forth like a bridegroom coming from his
tent,
rejoices like a champion to run his course.

[7] At one end of the heavens is the rising of the sun;
to its furthest end it runs its course.
There is nothing concealed from its burning heat.

*   *   *

[8] The law of the LORD is perfect;
it revives the soul.
The decrees of the LORD are steadfast;
they give wisdom to the simple.

⁹ The precepts of the LORD are right;
   they gladden the heart.
   The command of the LORD is clear;
   it gives light to the eyes.

¹⁰ The fear of the LORD is pure,
   abiding forever.
   The judgments of the LORD are true;
   they are, all of them, just.

¹¹ They are more to be desired than gold,
   than quantities of gold.
   And sweeter are they than honey,
   than honey flowing from the comb.

¹² So in them your servant finds instruction;
   great reward is in their keeping.
¹³ But who can detect their own errors?
   From hidden faults acquit me.

¹⁴ From presumption restrain your servant;
   may it not rule me.
   Then shall I be blameless,
   clean from grave sin.

¹⁵ May the spoken words of my mouth,
   the thoughts of my heart,
   win favor in your sight, O LORD,
   my rock and my redeemer!

Psalm 20 (19)

¹ *For the Choirmaster. A Psalm of David.*

² May the LORD answer you in time of trial;
  may the name of Jacob's God protect you.
³ May he send you help from the holy place,
  and give you support from Sion.

⁴ May he remember all your offerings,
  and receive your sacrifice with favor.
⁵ May he give you your heart's desire,
  and fulfill every one of your plans.

⁶ May we ring out our joy at your victory,
  and raise banners in the name of our God.
  May the LORD grant all your prayers.

⁷ Now I know the LORD saves his anointed,
  and answers from his holy heaven
  with the mighty victory of his hand.

⁸ Some put their trust in chariots or horses,
  but we in the name of the LORD, our God.
⁹ They will collapse and fall,
  but we shall rise up and hold firm.
¹⁰ Grant salvation to the king, O LORD,
  give answer on the day we call.

Psalm 21 (20)

¹ *For the Choirmaster. A Psalm of David.*

² In your strength, O LORD, the king rejoices;
  how greatly your salvation makes him glad!
³ You have granted him his heart's desire;
  you have not withheld the prayer of his lips.

⁴ You came to meet him with blessings of
      prosperity;
  you have set on his head a crown of pure gold.
⁵ He asked you for life and this you have given:
  days that will last from age to age.

⁶ By your saving help great is his glory;
  you have bestowed upon him majesty and
      splendor;
⁷ you have granted him blessings forever,
  made him rejoice with the joy of your presence.

⁸ The king has placed his trust in the LORD.
  Through the mercy of the Most High, he is
      unshaken.

⁹ Your hand will find out all your foes,
   your right hand will find out those that hate you.
¹⁰ You will burn them like a blazing furnace
   on the day when you appear,
   and the LORD will consume them in his anger:
   fire will swallow them up.

¹¹ You will wipe out their descendants from the
         earth,
   and their offspring from the human race.
¹² Though they planned evil against you,
   though they plotted, they shall not prevail.

¹³ For you will force them to retreat;
   at them you will aim with your bow.
¹⁴ O LORD, arise in your strength;
   we shall sing and praise your power.

Psalm 22 (21)

¹ *For the Choirmaster. In the manner of "The Doe at Daybreak." A Psalm of David.*

² My God, my God, why have you forsaken me?
Why are you far from saving me,
so far from my words of anguish?
³ O my God, I call by day and you do not answer;
I call by night and I find no reprieve.

⁴ Yet you, O God, are holy,
enthroned on the praises of Israel.
⁵ In you our forebears put their trust;
they trusted and you set them free.
⁶ When they cried to you, they escaped;
in you they trusted and were not put to shame.

⁷ But I am a worm and no man,
scorned by everyone, despised by the people.
⁸ All who see me deride me;
they curl their lips, they toss their heads:
⁹ "He trusted in the LORD, let him save him;
let him release him, for in him he delights."

¹⁰ Yes, it was you who took me from the womb,
entrusted me to my mother's breast.
¹¹ To you I was committed from birth;
from my mother's womb, you have been my God.
¹² Stay not far from me;
trouble is near, and there is no one to help.

¹³ Many bulls have surrounded me,
   fierce bulls of Bashan close me in.
¹⁴ Against me they open wide their mouths,
   like a lion, rending and roaring.

¹⁵ Like water I am poured out,
   disjointed are all my bones.
   My heart has become like wax,
   it is melted within my breast.

¹⁶ Parched as burnt clay is my throat,
   my tongue cleaves to my jaws.
   You lay me in the dust of death.
¹⁷ For dogs have surrounded me;
   a band of the wicked besets me.
   They tear holes in my hands and my feet;

¹⁸ I can count every one of my bones.
   They stare at me and gloat.
¹⁹ They divide my clothing among them,
   they cast lots for my robe.

²⁰ But you, O Lord, do not stay afar off;
   my strength, make haste to help me!
²¹ Rescue my soul from the sword,
   my life from the grip of the dog.
²² Save my life from the jaws of the lion,
   my poor soul from the horns of wild bulls.

²³ I will tell of your name to my kin,
  and praise you in the midst of the assembly;
²⁴ "You who fear the LORD, give him praise;
  all descendants of Jacob, give him glory;
  revere him, all you descendants of Israel.

²⁵ For he has never despised
  nor scorned the poverty of the poor.
  From him he has not hidden his face,
  but he heard him whenever he cried."

²⁶ You are my praise in the great assembly.
  My vows I will pay before those who fear him.
²⁷ The poor shall eat and shall have their fill.
  They shall praise the LORD, those who seek him.
  May their hearts live on forever and ever!

²⁸ All the earth shall remember and return to the
      LORD,
  all families of the nations worship before him,
²⁹ for the kingdom is the LORD's, he is ruler of the
      nations.
³⁰ They shall worship him, all the mighty of the
      earth;
  before him shall bow all who go down to the dust.

³¹ And my soul shall live for him, my descendants
      serve him.
  They shall tell of the LORD to generations yet to
      come,
³² declare his saving justice to peoples yet unborn:
  "These are the things the LORD has done."

Psalm 23 *(22)*

¹ *A Psalm of David.*

The LORD is my shepherd;
there is nothing I shall want.
² Fresh and green are the pastures
where he gives me repose.
Near restful waters he leads me;
³ he revives my soul.

He guides me along the right path,
for the sake of his name.
⁴ Though I should walk in the valley of the shadow
of death,
no evil would I fear, for you are with me.
Your crook and your staff will give me comfort.

⁵ You have prepared a table before me
in the sight of my foes.
My head you have anointed with oil;
my cup is overflowing.

⁶ Surely goodness and mercy shall follow me
all the days of my life.
In the LORD's own house shall I dwell
for length of days unending.

Psalm 24 *(23)*

¹ *A Psalm of David.*

The LORD's is the earth and its fullness,
the world, and those who dwell in it.
² It is he who set it on the seas;
on the rivers he made it firm.

³ Who shall climb the mountain of the LORD?
Who shall stand in his holy place?
⁴ The clean of hands and pure of heart,
whose soul is not set on vain things,
who has not sworn deceitful words.

⁵ Blessings from the LORD shall he receive,
and right reward from the God who saves him.
⁶ Such are the people who seek him,
who seek the face of the God of Jacob.

*   *   *

⁷ O gates, lift high your heads;
grow higher, ancient doors.
Let him enter, the king of glory!

[8] Who is this king of glory?
  The LORD, the mighty, the valiant;
  the LORD, the valiant in war.

[9] O gates, lift high your heads;
  grow higher, ancient doors.
  Let him enter, the king of glory!

[10] Who is this king of glory?
  He, the LORD of hosts,
  he is the king of glory.

Psalm 25 *(24)*

¹ *Of David.*

To you, O Lord, I lift up my soul.
² In you, O my God, I have trusted;
let me not be put to shame;
let not my enemies exult over me.
³ Let none who hope in you be put to shame;
but shamed are those who wantonly break faith.

⁴ O Lord, make me know your ways.
Teach me your paths.
⁵ Guide me in your truth, and teach me;
for you are the God of my salvation.
I have hoped in you all day long.

⁶ Remember your compassion, O Lord,
and your merciful love,
for they are from of old.

⁷ Do not remember the sins of my youth,
nor my transgressions.
In your merciful love remember me,
because of your goodness, O Lord.

⁸ Good and upright is the Lord;
he shows the way to sinners.
⁹ He guides the humble in right judgment;
to the humble he teaches his way.

¹⁰ All the LORD's paths are mercy and faithfulness,
for those who keep his covenant and commands.
¹¹ O LORD, for the sake of your name,
forgive my guilt, for it is great.

¹² Who is this that fears the LORD?
He will show him the path to choose.
¹³ His soul shall live in happiness,
and his descendants shall possess the land.
¹⁴ The LORD's secret is for those who fear him;
to them he reveals his covenant.

¹⁵ My eyes are always on the LORD,
for he rescues my feet from the snare.
¹⁶ Turn to me and have mercy on me,
for I am alone and poor.

¹⁷ Relieve the anguish of my heart,
and set me free from my distress.
¹⁸ See my lowliness and suffering,
and take away all my sins.

¹⁹ See how many are my foes;
with a violent hatred they hate me.
²⁰ Preserve my life and rescue me.
Let me not be put to shame,
for in you I trust.

²¹ May integrity and virtue protect me,
for I have hoped in you, O LORD.
²² Redeem Israel, O God,
from all its distress.

Psalm 26 (25)

¹ *Of David.*

Give judgment for me, O LORD,
for I have walked in my integrity.
I have trusted in the LORD; I have not wavered.

² Examine me, LORD, and try me.
O test my heart and my mind.
³ Your mercy is before my eyes,
and I walk according to your truth.

⁴ I never take my seat with liars,
and with hypocrites I shall not go.
⁵ I hate the evildoer's company;
I will not take my seat with the wicked.

⁶ I wash my hands in innocence
  and take my place around your altar,
⁷ singing a song of thanksgiving,
  recounting all your wonders.
⁸ O LORD, I love the house where you dwell,
  the place where your glory abides.

⁹ Do not sweep away my soul with sinners,
  nor my life with those who shed blood,
¹⁰ in whose hands are evil plots,
  whose right hands are filled with a bribe.

¹¹ As for me, I have walked in my integrity.
  Redeem me and have mercy on me.
¹² My foot stands on level ground:
  I will bless the LORD in the assembly.

Psalm 27 (26)

[1] *Of David.*

The LORD is my light and my salvation;
whom shall I fear?
The LORD is the stronghold of my life;
whom should I dread?

[2] When those who do evil draw near
to devour my flesh,
it is they, my enemies and foes,
who stumble and fall.

[3] Though an army encamp against me,
my heart would not fear.
Though war break out against me,
even then would I trust.

[4] There is one thing I ask of the LORD,
only this do I seek:
to live in the house of the LORD
all the days of my life,
to gaze on the beauty of the LORD,
to inquire at his temple.

[5] For there he keeps me safe in his shelter
in the day of evil.
He hides me under cover of his tent;
he sets me high upon a rock.

6 And now my head shall be raised
above my foes who surround me,
and I shall offer within his tent
a sacrifice of joy.
I will sing and make music for the LORD.

7 O LORD, hear my voice when I call;
have mercy and answer me.
8 Of you my heart has spoken,
"Seek his face."

It is your face, O LORD, that I seek;
9 hide not your face from me.
Dismiss not your servant in anger;
you have been my help.

Do not abandon or forsake me,
O God, my Savior!
10 Though father and mother forsake me,
the LORD will receive me.

11 Instruct me, LORD, in your way;
on an even path lead me
because of my enemies.
12 Do not leave me to the will of my foes,
for false witnesses rise up against me,
and they breathe out violence.

13 I believe I shall see the LORD's goodness
in the land of the living.
14 Wait for the LORD; be strong;
be stouthearted, and wait for the LORD!

Psalm 28 *(27)*

¹ *Of David.*

To you, O LORD, I call;
my rock, be not deaf to me.
I shall go down to those in the pit,
if you are silent to me.

² Hear the voice of my pleading
as I call to you for help,
as I raise my hands
toward your holy place.

³ Do not drag me away with the wicked,
with those who do evil,
who speak words of peace to their neighbors,
but with malice in their hearts.

⁴ Repay them according to their deeds,
according to the evil of their actions.
According to their handiwork, repay them;
return to them their deserts.

⁵ For they ignore the deeds of the LORD
 and the work of his hands.
 May he ruin them and never rebuild them.
⁶ Blest be the LORD, for he has heard
 the sound of my appeal.

⁷ The LORD is my strength and my shield;
 in him my heart trusts.
 I was helped; my heart rejoices,
 and I praise him with my song.

⁸ The LORD is the strength of his people,
 a saving refuge for his anointed.
⁹ Save your people and bless your heritage.
 Shepherd them and carry them forever.

Psalm 29 (28)

Ascribe to the LORD, you heavenly powers,
ascribe to the LORD glory and strength.
² Ascribe to the LORD the glory of his name;
bow down before the LORD, majestic in holiness.

³ The voice of the LORD upon the waters,
the God of glory thunders;
the LORD on the immensity of waters;
⁴ the voice of the LORD full of power;
the voice of the LORD full of splendor.

⁵ The voice of the LORD shatters cedars,
the LORD shatters the cedars of Lebanon;
⁶ he makes Lebanon leap like a calf,
and Sirion like a young wild-ox.

⁷ The voice of the LORD flashes flames of fire.
⁸ The voice of the LORD shakes the wilderness,
the LORD shakes the wilderness of Kadesh;
⁹ the voice of the LORD rends the oak tree
and strips the forest bare.
In his temple they all cry, "Glory!"

¹⁰ The LORD sat enthroned above the flood;
the LORD sits as king forever.
¹¹ The LORD will give strength to his people,
the LORD will bless his people with peace.

Psalm 30 (29)

¹ *A Psalm. A Canticle for the Dedication of the*
   Temple. Of David.

² I will extol you, LORD, for you have raised me up,
   and have not let my enemies rejoice over me.

³ O LORD my God, I cried to you for help,
   and you have healed me.
⁴ O LORD, you have lifted up my soul from the
         grave,
   restored me to life from those who sink into the
         pit.

⁵ Sing psalms to the LORD, you faithful ones;
   give thanks to his holy name.
⁶ His anger lasts a moment; his favor all through
         life.
   At night come tears, but dawn brings joy.

⁷ I said to myself in my good fortune:
   "I shall never be shaken."
⁸ O LORD, your favor had set me like a mountain
         stronghold.
   Then you hid your face, and I was put to
         confusion.

⁹ To you, O LORD, I cried,
   to my God I appealed for mercy:
¹⁰ "What profit is my lifeblood, my going to the
         grave?
   Can dust give you thanks, or proclaim your
         faithfulness?"

¹¹ Hear, O LORD, and have mercy on me;
   be my helper, O LORD.
¹² You have changed my mourning into dancing,
   removed my sackcloth and girded me with joy.
¹³ So my soul sings psalms to you, and will not be
         silent.
   O LORD my God, I will thank you forever.

Psalm 31 (30)

¹ *For the Choirmaster. A Psalm of David.*

² In you, O LORD, I take refuge.
  Let me never be put to shame.
  In your justice, set me free;
³ incline your ear to me, and speedily rescue me.

  Be a rock of refuge for me,
  a mighty stronghold to save me.
⁴ For you are my rock, my stronghold!
  Lead me, guide me, for the sake of your name.

⁵ Release me from the snare they have hidden,
  for you indeed are my refuge.
⁶ Into your hands I commend my spirit.
  You will redeem me, O LORD, O faithful God.
⁷ You detest those who serve empty idols.
  As for me, I trust in the LORD.

⁸ Let me be glad and rejoice in your mercy,
  for you who have seen my affliction
  and taken heed of my soul's distress,
⁹ have not left me in the hands of the enemy,
  but set my feet at large.

¹⁰ Have mercy on me, O LORD,
   for I am in distress.
   My eyes are wasted with grief,
   my soul and my body.

¹¹ For my life is spent with sorrow,
   and my years with sighs.
   Affliction has broken down my strength,
   and my bones waste away.

¹² Because of all my foes
   I have become a reproach,
   an object of scorn to my neighbors
   and of fear to my friends.

   Those who see me in the street
   flee from me.
¹³ I am forgotten, like someone dead,
   and have become like a broken vessel.

¹⁴ I have heard the slander of the crowd;
   terror all around me,
   as they plot together against me,
   as they plan to take my life.

¹⁵ But as for me, I trust in you, O LORD;
   I say, "You are my God.
¹⁶ My lot is in your hands, deliver me
   from the hands of my enemies
   and those who pursue me.

¹⁷ Let your face shine on your servant.
  Save me in your merciful love.
¹⁸ Let me not be put to shame, O LORD,
  for I call on you;
  let the wicked be shamed!
  Let them be silenced in the grave!

¹⁹ Let lying lips be stilled,
  that speak haughtily against the just man
  with pride and contempt."

²⁰ How great is the goodness, LORD,
  that you keep for those who fear you,
  that you show to those who trust you
  in the sight of the children of men.

²¹ You hide them in the shelter of your presence,
  secure from human scheming;
  you keep them safe within your tent
  from disputing tongues.

²² Blest be the LORD for he has wondrously shown
      me
  his merciful love in a fortified city!

²³ "I am far removed from your sight,"
  I said in my alarm.
  Yet you heard the voice of my plea
  when I cried to you for help.

²⁴ Love the LORD, all you his saints.
  The LORD guards the faithful.
  But the LORD will repay to the full
  the one who acts with pride.
²⁵ Be strong, let your heart take courage,
  all who hope in the LORD.

Psalm 32 *(31)*

¹ *Of David. A* Maskil.

Blessed is he whose transgression is forgiven,
whose sin is remitted.
² Blessed the man to whom the LORD imputes no
      guilt,
in whose spirit is no guile.

³ I kept it secret and my frame was wasted.
I groaned all day long,
⁴ for your hand, by day and by night,
lay heavy upon me.
Indeed, my strength was dried up
as by the summer's heat.

⁵ To you I have acknowledged my sin;
my guilt I did not hide.
I said, "I will confess my transgression to the
      LORD."
And you have forgiven the guilt of my sin.

⁶ So let each faithful one pray to you
in the time of need.
The floods of water may reach high,
but such a one they shall not reach.

7 You are a hiding place for me;
   you keep me safe from distress;
   you surround me with cries of deliverance.

8 I will instruct you and teach you
   the way you should go;
   I will fix my eyes upon you.

9 Be not like horse and mule, unintelligent,
   needing bridle and bit,
   or else they will not approach you.

10 Many sorrows has the wicked,
   but loving mercy surrounds
   one who trusts in the Lord.

11 Rejoice in the Lord; exult, you just!
   Ring out your joy, all you upright of heart!

Psalm 33 (32)

¹ Ring out your joy to the LORD, O you just;
   for praise is fitting for the upright.
² Give thanks to the LORD upon the harp;
   with a ten-stringed lute sing him songs.
³ O sing him a song that is new;
   play skillfully, with shouts of joy.

⁴ For the word of the LORD is faithful,
   and all his works to be trusted.
⁵ The LORD loves justice and right,
   and his merciful love fills the earth.

⁶ By the word of the LORD the heavens were made,
   by the breath of his mouth all their host.
⁷ As in a flask, he collects the waves of the ocean;
   he stores up the depths of the sea.

⁸ Let all the earth fear the LORD,
   all who live in the world revere him.
⁹ He spoke, and it came to be.
   He commanded; it stood in place.

¹⁰ The LORD frustrates the designs of the nations;
   he defeats the plans of the peoples.
¹¹ The designs of the LORD stand forever,
   the plans of his heart from age to age.

¹² Blessed the nation whose God is the LORD,
the people he has chosen as his heritage.
¹³ From the heavens the Lord looks forth;
he sees all the children of men.

¹⁴ From the place where he dwells he gazes
on all the dwellers on the earth,
¹⁵ he who shapes the hearts of them all,
and considers all their deeds.

¹⁶ A king is not saved by his great army,
nor a warrior preserved by his great strength.
¹⁷ A vain hope for safety is the horse;
despite its power it cannot save.

¹⁸ Yes, the LORD's eyes are on those who fear him,
who hope in his merciful love,
¹⁹ to rescue their souls from death,
to keep them alive in famine.

²⁰ Our soul is waiting for the LORD.
He is our help and our shield.
²¹ In him do our hearts find joy.
We trust in his holy name.
²² May your merciful love be upon us,
as we hope in you, O LORD.

Psalm 34 (33)

¹ *Of David, when he feigned madness before*
   Abimelech, so that he drove him out,
   and he went away.

² I will bless the LORD at all times;
   praise of him is always in my mouth.
³ In the LORD my soul shall make its boast;
   the humble shall hear and be glad.

⁴ Glorify the LORD with me;
   together let us praise his name.
⁵ I sought the LORD, and he answered me;
   from all my terrors he set me free.

⁶ Look toward him and be radiant;
   let your faces not be abashed.
⁷ This lowly one called; the LORD heard,
   and rescued him from all his distress.

⁸ The angel of the LORD is encamped
   around those who fear him, to rescue them.
⁹ Taste and see that the LORD is good.
   Blessed the man who seeks refuge in him.

¹⁰ Fear the LORD, you his holy ones.
   They lack nothing, those who fear him.
¹¹ The rich suffer want and go hungry,
   but those who seek the LORD lack no blessing.

¹² Come, children, and hear me,
   that I may teach you the fear of the Lord.
¹³ Who is it that desires life
   and longs to see prosperous days?

¹⁴ Guard your tongue from evil,
   and your lips from speaking deceit.
¹⁵ Turn aside from evil and do good.
   Seek after peace, and pursue it.

¹⁶ The Lord turns his eyes to the just,
   and his ears are open to their cry.
¹⁷ The Lord turns his face against the wicked
   to destroy their remembrance from the earth.

¹⁸ When the just cry out, the Lord hears,
   and rescues them in all their distress.
¹⁹ The Lord is close to the brokenhearted;
   those whose spirit is crushed he will save.

²⁰ Many are the trials of the just man,
   but from them all the Lord will rescue him.
²¹ He will keep guard over all his bones;
   not one of his bones shall be broken.

²² Evil brings death to the wicked;
   those who hate the just man are doomed.
²³ The Lord ransoms the souls of his servants.
   All who trust in him shall not be condemned.

Psalm 35 (34)

[1] *Of David.*

Contend, O Lord, with my contenders;
fight those who fight me.
[2] Take up your buckler and shield;
arise in my defense.

[3] Take up the javelin and the spear
against those who pursue me.
Say to my soul, "I am your salvation."

[4] Let those who seek my life
be shamed and disgraced.
Let those who plan evil against me
be routed in confusion.

[5] Let them be like chaff before the wind;
let the Lord's angel trip them up.
[6] Let their path be slippery and dark;
let the Lord's angel pursue them.

⁷ Unprovoked, they have hidden a net for me;
   they have dug a pit for me.
⁸ Let ruin fall upon them,
   and take them by surprise.
   Let them be caught in the net they have hidden;
   let them fall in their own pit.

⁹ Then my soul shall rejoice in the LORD,
   and exult in his salvation.
¹⁰ All my bones will say,
   "LORD, who is like you
   who rescue the weak from the strong
   and the poor from the oppressor?"

¹¹ Lying witnesses arise,
   asking me questions I cannot understand.
¹² They repay me evil for good;
   my soul is forlorn.

¹³ When they were sick I dressed in sackcloth,
   afflicted my soul with fasting,
   and with prayer ever anew in my heart,
¹⁴ as for a brother, a friend.
   I went as though mourning a mother,
   bowed down with grief.

¹⁵ Now that I stumble, they gladly gather;
   they gather, and mock me.
   I myself do not know them,
   yet strangers tear at me ceaselessly.
¹⁶ They provoke me with mockery on mockery,
   and gnash their teeth at me.

¹⁷ O Lᴏʀᴅ, how long will you look on?
   Rescue my life from their ravages,
   my soul from these lions.
¹⁸ Then I will thank you in the great assembly;
   amid the mighty throng I will praise you.

¹⁹ Do not let my lying foes
   rejoice over me.
   Do not let those who hate me without cause
   wink eyes at each other.

²⁰ They speak no peace to the quiet ones
   who live in the land.
   Rather, they make deceitful plots,
²¹ and, with mouths wide open,
   they utter their cry against me:
   "Yes, yes! Our eyes have seen it!"

²² O Lᴏʀᴅ, you have seen; do not be silent;
   Lord, do not stand afar off!
²³ Awake! And stir to my defense,
   to my cause, O my God and my Lord!

²⁴ Vindicate me, LORD, my God,
    in accord with your justice;
    and let them not rejoice over me.

²⁵ Do not let them think in their hearts,
    "Yes, we have won."
    Do not let them say,
    "We have destroyed him!"

²⁶ Let them be shamed and brought to disgrace
    who rejoice at my misfortune.
    Let them be covered with shame and confusion
    who raise themselves against me.

²⁷ Let them exult and be glad
    who delight in my deliverance.
    Let them say without end,
    "Great is the LORD who delights
    in the peace of his servant."

²⁸ Then my tongue shall speak of your justice,
    and all day long of your praise.

Psalm 36 (35)

¹ *For the Choirmaster. Of David, the servant of the*
  Lord.

² Transgression speaks to the sinner
  in the depths of his heart.
  There is no fear of God
  before his eyes.

³ In his own eyes, he flatters himself,
  not to see and detest his own guilt.
⁴ The words of his mouth are mischief and deceit.
  He has ceased to be prudent and do good.

⁵ In bed he plots iniquity.
  He sets his foot on every wicked way;
  no evil does he reject.

⁶ Your mercy, Lord, reaches to heaven,
  your truth to the clouds.
⁷ Your justice is like God's mountains;
  like the great deep, your justice.
  Both man and beast you save, O Lord.

8 How precious is your mercy, O God!
  The children of men seek shelter
  in the shadow of your wings.

9 They feast on the riches of your house;
  you give them drink from the stream of your
          delight.
10 For with you is the fountain of life,
  and in your light we see light.

11 Maintain your mercy for those who know you,
  your saving justice to upright hearts.
12 Let the foot of the proud not tread on me
  nor the hand of the wicked drive me out.
13 There have the evildoers fallen;
  flung down, unable to rise!

Psalm 37 (36)

¹ *Of David.*

Do not fret because of the wicked;
do not envy those who do evil,
² for they wither quickly like grass
and fade like the green of the fields.

³ Trust in the LORD and do good;
then you will dwell in the land and safely pasture.
⁴ Find your delight in the LORD,
who grants your heart's desire.

⁵ Commit your way to the LORD;
trust in him, and he will act,
⁶ and make your uprightness shine like the light,
the justice of your cause like the noonday sun.

⁷ Be still before the LORD and wait in patience;
do not fret at the one who prospers,
the one who makes evil plots.

⁸ Calm your anger and forget your rage;
do not fret, it only leads to evil.
⁹ For those who do evil shall perish.
But those who hope in the LORD,
they shall inherit the land.

¹⁰ A little longer—and the wicked one is gone.
Look at his place: he is not there.
¹¹ But the humble shall own the land
and delight in fullness of peace.

¹² The wicked one plots against the just man
and gnashes his teeth against him;
¹³ but the LORD laughs at the wicked,
for he sees that his day is at hand.

¹⁴ The wicked draw the sword, bend their bows,
to slaughter the poor and needy,
to slay those whose ways are upright.
¹⁵ Their sword shall pierce their own hearts,
and their bows shall be broken to pieces.

¹⁶ Better the few possessions of the just,
than the abundant wealth of the wicked;
¹⁷ for the arms of the wicked shall be broken,
and the LORD will support the just.

¹⁸ The LORD takes note of the days of the blameless;
their heritage will last forever.
¹⁹ They shall not be put to shame in evil days;
in time of famine they shall have their fill.

²⁰ But all the wicked shall perish;
the enemies of the LORD shall be consumed.
They are like the beauty of the meadows;
they shall vanish, they shall vanish like smoke.

²¹ The wicked borrows and does not repay,
    but the upright is generous and gives.
²² Those blessed by him shall inherit the land,
    but those cursed by him shall be cut off.

²³ By the LORD are the steps made firm
    of one in whose path He delights.
²⁴ Though he stumble he shall never fall,
    for the LORD will hold him by the hand.

²⁵ I was young and now I am old,
    but I have never seen the just man forsaken
    nor his children begging for bread.
²⁶ All the day he is generous and lends,
    and his children become a blessing.

²⁷ Then turn away from evil and do good,
    and you may abide forever;
²⁸ for indeed, the LORD loves justice,
    and will never forsake his faithful.

The unjust shall be wiped out forever,
    and the descendants of the wicked destroyed.
²⁹ The just shall inherit the land;
    there they shall abide forever.

³⁰ The mouth of the just man utters wisdom,
    and his tongue tells forth what is just.
³¹ The law of his God is in his heart;
    his steps shall be saved from stumbling.

³² The wicked man keeps watch for the just,
  and seeks an occasion to destroy him.
³³ The LORD will not leave him in his power,
  nor let him be condemned when he is judged.

³⁴ Then wait for the LORD, keep to his way.
  He will exalt you to inherit the land,
  and you will see the wicked destroyed.

³⁵ I have seen the wicked one triumphant,
  towering like a cedar of Lebanon.
³⁶ I passed by again; he was gone.
  I searched; he was nowhere to be found.

³⁷ Mark the blameless, observe the upright;
  for the peaceful man a future lies in store,
³⁸ but sinners shall all be destroyed.
  No future lies in store for the wicked.

³⁹ But from the LORD comes the salvation of the
        just,
  their stronghold in time of distress.
⁴⁰ The LORD helps them and rescues them,
  rescues and saves them from the wicked:
  because they take refuge in him.

Psalm 38 (37)

¹ *A Psalm of David. For a Memorial.*

² O LORD, do not rebuke me in your anger;
 reprove me not in your rage.
³ For your arrows have sunk deep in me;
 your hand has come down upon me.

⁴ There is no soundness in my flesh
 because of your anger:
 there is no health in my limbs
 because of my sin.

⁵ My guilt towers higher than my head;
 it is a weight too heavy to bear.
⁶ My wounds are foul and festering,
 the result of my own folly.
⁷ I am bowed and brought to my knees.
 I go mourning all the day long.

⁸ All my frame is burning with fever;
 there is no soundness in my flesh.
⁹ I am spent and utterly crushed,
 I cry aloud in anguish of heart.

¹⁰ O Lord, all my longing lies before you;
 my groans are not hidden from you.
¹¹ My heart throbs, my strength is spent;
 the very light has gone from my eyes.

¹² Friends and companions stand aloof from my
        pain;
    those closest to me stand afar off.
¹³ Those who plot against my life lay snares;
    those who seek my ruin speak of harm,
    planning treachery all the day long.

¹⁴ But I, like someone deaf, do not hear;
    like someone mute, I do not open my mouth.
¹⁵ I am like one who hears nothing,
    in whose mouth is no defense.

¹⁶ But in you, O Lord, I hope;
    it is you, Lord my God, who will answer.
¹⁷ I pray, "Let them not gloat over me,
    exult if my foot should slip."

¹⁸ For I am on the point of falling,
    and my pain is always with me.
¹⁹ I confess that I am guilty;
    and I am grieved because of my sin.

²⁰ My wanton enemies live on and grow strong,
    and many are my lying foes.
²¹ They repay me evil for good,
    and attack me for seeking what is good.

²² Forsake me not, O Lord!
    My God, be not far from me!
²³ Make haste and come to my help,
    my Lord and my salvation!

Psalm 39 (38)

¹ *For the Choirmaster, for Jeduthun. A Psalm of David.*

² I said, "I will be watchful of my ways,
   for fear I should sin with my tongue.
   I will put a curb on my lips
   when the wicked man stands before me."
³ I was mute, silent, very still,
   as my pain became intense.

⁴ My heart was burning within me.
   At the thought of it, the fire blazed up,
   and my tongue burst into speech:
⁵ "O LORD, you have shown me my end,
   how short is the length of my days.
   Now I know how fleeting is my life.

⁶ How short the span of days you have given me;
   my life is as nothing in your sight.
   Surely all mankind stands as but a breath.
⁷ A man surely lives as a shadow,
   surely the riches he hoards, a mere breath;
   he does not know who will gather them."

8 And now, Lord, what is there to wait for?
  In you rests all my hope.
9 Set me free from all my sins;
  do not make me the taunt of the fool.
10 I was silent, not opening my lips,
  because this was all your doing.

11 Take away your scourge from me.
  I am crushed by the blows of your hand.
12 With rebukes you correct the sinner;
  like a moth you devour all he treasures.
  All mankind is no more than a breath.

13 O LORD, give heed to my prayer;
  turn your ear to my cry;
  do not be deaf to my weeping.
  Behold, I am a stranger to you,
  a pilgrim, like all my forebears.

14 Look away from me that I may smile
  before I depart to be no more.

Psalm 40 (39)

¹ *For the Choirmaster. Of David. A Psalm.*

² I waited, I waited for the LORD,
  and he stooped down to me;
  he heard my cry.

³ He drew me from the deadly pit,
  from the miry clay.
  He set my feet upon a rock,
  made my footsteps firm.

⁴ He put a new song into my mouth,
  praise of our God.
  Many shall see and fear
  and shall trust in the LORD.

⁵ Blessed the man who has placed
  his trust in the LORD,
  and has not gone over to the proud
  who follow false gods.

⁶ How many, O LORD my God,
  are the wonders and designs
  that you have worked for us;
  you have no equal.
  Should I wish to proclaim or speak of them,
  they would be more than I can tell!

⁷ You delight not in sacrifice and offerings,
  but in an open ear.
  You do not ask for holocaust and victim.

⁸ Then I said, "See, I have come."
  In the scroll of the book it stands written of me:
⁹ "I delight to do your will, O my God;
  your instruction lies deep within me."

¹⁰ Your justice I have proclaimed
   in the great assembly.
   My lips I have not sealed;
   you know it, O Lord.

¹¹ Your saving help I have not hidden in my heart;
   of your faithfulness and salvation I have spoken.
   I made no secret of your merciful love
   and your faithfulness to the great assembly.

¹² O Lord, you will not withhold
   your compassion from me.
   Your merciful love and your faithfulness
   will always guard me.

¹³ For I am beset with evils
   too many to be counted.
   My iniquities have overtaken me,
   till I can see no more.
   They are more than the hairs of my head,
   and my heart is sinking.

¹⁴ Be pleased, O Lᴏʀᴅ, to rescue me;
   Lᴏʀᴅ, make haste to help me.
¹⁵ O let there be shame and confusion
   on those who seek my life.

   O let them turn back in confusion
   who delight in my harm.
¹⁶ Let them be appalled because of their shame,
   those who jeer and mock me.

¹⁷ O let there be rejoicing and gladness
   for all who seek you.
   Let them ever say, "The Lᴏʀᴅ is great,"
   who long for your salvation.

¹⁸ Wretched and poor though I am,
   the Lord is mindful of me.
   You are my rescuer, my help;
   O my God, do not delay.

Psalm 41 (40)

¹ *For the Choirmaster. A Psalm of David.*

² Blessed is he who has concern for the poor.
   In time of trouble, the Lᴏʀᴅ will rescue him.

³ The Lᴏʀᴅ will guard him, give him life,
   and make him blessed in the land,
   not give him up to the will of his foes.

⁴ The LORD will help him on his bed of pain;
   you will bring him back from sickness to health.

⁵ As for me, I said, "LORD, have mercy on me;
   heal my soul, for I have sinned against you."
⁶ My foes are speaking evil against me:
   "How long before he dies, and his name be
         forgotten?"
⁷ When someone comes to visit me, he speaks
         empty words;
   his heart stores up malice; on leaving, he spreads lies.

⁸ All my foes whisper together against me;
   they devise evil plots against me:
⁹ "Something deadly has fastened upon him;
   he will not rise from where he lies."

¹⁰ Thus even my friend, in whom I trusted,
   who ate my bread,
      has lifted his heel against me.

¹¹ But you, O LORD, have mercy on me.
   Raise me up and I will repay them.
¹² By this I know your favor:
   that my foes do not triumph over me.
¹³ In my integrity you have upheld me,
   and have set me in your presence forever.

*   *   *

[14] Blest be the LORD, the God of Israel,
   from age to age. Amen. Amen.

BOOK TWO
Of The Psalter

Psalm 42 (41)

¹ *For the Choirmaster. A* Maskil. *Of the sons of Korah.*

² Like the deer that yearns
   for running streams,
   so my soul is yearning
   for you, my God.

³ My soul is thirsting for God,
   the living God;
   when can I enter and appear
   before the face of God?

⁴ My tears have become my bread,
   by day, by night,
   as they say to me all the day long,
   "Where is your God?"

⁵ These things will I remember
   as I pour out my soul:
   for I would go to the place
   of your wondrous tent,
   all the way to the house of God,
   amid cries of gladness and thanksgiving,
   the throng keeping joyful festival.

⁶ Why are you cast down, my soul;
  why groan within me?
  Hope in God; I will praise him yet again,
  my saving presence and my God.

⁷ My soul is cast down within me,
  therefore I remember you
  from the land of Jordan and Mount Hermon,
  from the Hill of Mizar.

⁸ Deep is calling on deep,
  in the roar of your torrents;
  your billows and all your waves
  swept over me.

⁹ By day the LORD decrees
  his merciful love;
  by night his song is with me,
  prayer to the God of my life.

¹⁰ I will say to God, my rock,
   "Why have you forgotten me?
   Why do I go mourning
   oppressed by the foe?"

¹¹ With a deadly wound in my bones,
   my enemies revile me,
   saying to me all the day long,
   "Where is your God?"

¹² Why are you cast down, my soul;
   why groan within me?
   Hope in God; I will praise him yet again,
   my saving presence and my God.

Psalm 43 *(42)*

¹ Give me justice, O God, and plead my cause
against a nation that is faithless.
From the deceitful and the cunning
rescue me, O God.

² You, O God, are my strength;
why have you rejected me?
Why do I go mourning,
oppressed by the foe?

³ O send forth your light and your truth;
they will guide me on.
They will bring me to your holy mountain,
to the place where you dwell.

⁴ And I will come to the altar of God,
to God, my joy and gladness.
To you will I give thanks on the harp,
O God, my God.

⁵ Why are you cast down, my soul;
why groan within me?
Hope in God; I will praise him yet again,
my saving presence and my God.

Psalm 44 (43)

¹ *For the Choirmaster. Of the sons of Korah.*
A Maskil.

² We heard with our own ears, O God;
   our forebears have declared to us
   the things you did in their days,
   you yourself, in days long ago.

³ With your own hand you drove out the nations,
   but them you planted;
   you brought affliction on the peoples;
   but them you set free.

⁴ No sword of their own won the land;
   no arm of their own brought them victory.
   It was your right hand and your arm,
   and the light of your face, for you loved them.

⁵ You are my king, O God;
   you command the victories for Jacob.
⁶ Through you we beat down our foes;
   in your name we trampled our aggressors.

⁷ For it was not in my bow that I trusted,
nor yet was I saved by my sword:
⁸ it was you who saved us from our foes;
those who hate us, you put to shame.
⁹ All day long our boast was in God,
and we will praise your name forever.

¹⁰ Yet now you have rejected us, disgraced us;
you no longer go forth with our armies.
¹¹ You make us retreat from the foe;
those who hate us plunder us at will.

¹² You make us like sheep for the slaughter,
and scatter us among the nations.
¹³ You sell your own people for nothing,
and make no profit by the sale.

¹⁴ You make us the taunt of our neighbors,
the mockery and scorn of those around us.
¹⁵ Among the nations you make us a byword;
among the peoples they shake their heads.

¹⁶ All day long my disgrace is before me;
my face is covered with shame
¹⁷ at the voice of the taunter, the scoffer,
at the sight of the foe and avenger.

¹⁸ This befell us though we had not forgotten you;
    we were not false to your covenant.
¹⁹ We had not withdrawn our hearts;
    our feet had not strayed from your path.
²⁰ Yet you have crushed us in a haunt of jackals,
    and covered us with the shadow of death.

²¹ Had we forgotten the name of our God,
    or stretched out our hands to a strange god,
²² would not God have found this out,
    he who knows the secrets of the heart?
²³ It is for you we are slain all day long,
    and are counted as sheep for the slaughter.

²⁴ Awake, O Lord! Why do you sleep?
    Arise! Do not reject us forever.
²⁵ Why do you hide your face,
    and forget our oppression and misery?

²⁶ For our soul is brought low to the dust;
    our body lies prostrate on the earth.
²⁷ Stand up and come to our help!
    Redeem us with your merciful love!

Psalm 45 (44)

¹ *For the Choirmaster. Intoned like "The Lilies."*
  Of the sons of Korah. A Maskil. *A Love Song.*

² My heart overflows with noble words.
  To the king I address the song I have made,
  my tongue as nimble as the pen of a scribe.

³ You are the most handsome of the sons of men,
  and graciousness is poured out upon your lips,
  for God has blessed you forevermore.

⁴ Gird your sword upon your thigh, O mighty one,
  with your splendor and your majesty.
⁵ In your majesty ride on triumphant
  in the cause of truth, meekness, and justice.
  May your right hand show your wondrous deeds.

⁶ Your arrows are sharp—peoples fall beneath you—
  in the heart of the foes of the king.

⁷ Your throne, O God, shall endure forever.
  A scepter of justice is the scepter of your kingdom.
⁸ Your love is for justice; your hatred for evil.

  Therefore God, your God, has anointed you
  with the oil of gladness above other kings:
⁹ your robes are fragrant with aloes, myrrh, and cassia.
  From the ivory palace you are gladdened with
      music.

¹⁰ The daughters of kings are those whom you
      favor.
On your right stands the queen in gold of Ophir.

¹¹ Listen, O daughter; pay heed and give ear:
forget your own people and your father's house.
¹² So will the king desire your beauty.
He is your lord, pay homage to him.

¹³ And the daughter of Tyre shall come with gifts;
the richest of the people shall seek your favor.
¹⁴ The daughter of the king is clothed with
      splendor;
her robes are threaded with gold.

¹⁵ In fine clothing she is led to the king;
behind her are her maiden companions, brought
      to you.
¹⁶ They are escorted amid gladness and joy;
they pass within the palace of the king.

¹⁷ Sons will be yours to succeed your fathers;
you will make them rulers over all the earth.
¹⁸ I will make your name forever remembered.
Thus the peoples will praise you from age to age.

Psalm 46 (45)

[1] *For the Choirmaster. Of the sons of Korah. Intoned like "The Maidens." A Song.*

[2] God is for us a refuge and strength,
   an ever-present help in time of distress:
[3] so we shall not fear though the earth should rock,
   though the mountains quake to the heart of the sea;
[4] even though its waters rage and foam,
   even though the mountains be shaken by its
         tumult.

The LORD of hosts is with us:
the God of Jacob is our stronghold.

[5] The waters of a river give joy to God's city,
   the holy place, the dwelling of the Most High.
[6] God is within, it cannot be shaken;
   God will help it at the dawning of the day.
[7] Nations are in tumult, kingdoms are shaken:
   he lifts his voice, the earth melts away.

⁸ The Lᴏʀᴅ of hosts is with us:
the God of Jacob is our stronghold.

⁹ Come and behold the works of the Lᴏʀᴅ,
the awesome deeds he has done on the earth.
¹⁰ He puts an end to wars over all the earth;
the bow he breaks, the spear he snaps, the shields
he burns with fire:
¹¹ "Be still and know that I am God,
exalted over nations, exalted over earth!"

¹² The Lᴏʀᴅ of hosts is with us:
the God of Jacob is our stronghold.

Psalm 47 (46)

¹ *For the Choirmaster. Of the sons of Korah. A Psalm.*

² All peoples, clap your hands.
  Cry to God with shouts of joy!
³ For the LORD, the Most High, is awesome,
  the great king over all the earth.

⁴ He humbles peoples under us
  and nations under our feet.
⁵ Our heritage he chose for us,
  the pride of Jacob whom he loves.

⁶ God goes up with shouts of joy.
  The LORD goes up with trumpet blast.
⁷ Sing praise for God; sing praise!
  Sing praise to our king; sing praise!

⁸ God is king of all the earth.
  Sing praise with all your skill.
⁹ God reigns over the nations.
  God sits upon his holy throne.

¹⁰ The princes of the peoples are assembled
  with the people of the God of Abraham.
  The rulers of the earth belong to God,
  who is greatly exalted.

Psalm 48 (47)

¹ *A Song. A Psalm. Of the sons of Korah.*

² Great is the LORD and highly to be praised
   in the city of our God.
³ His holy mountain rises in beauty,
   the joy of all the earth.

   Mount Sion, in the heart of the North,
   the city of the Mighty King!
⁴ God, in the midst of its citadels,
   has shown himself its stronghold.

⁵ Behold! the kings assembled;
   together they advanced.
⁶ They saw; at once they marveled;
   dismayed, they fled in fear.

⁷ A trembling seized them there,
   anguish, like pangs in giving birth,
⁸ as when the east wind shatters
   the ships of Tarshish.

⁹ As we have heard, so we have seen
   in the city of our God,
   in the city of the LORD of hosts,
   which God establishes forever.

¹⁰ Your merciful love, O God,
   we ponder in your temple.
¹¹ Your praise, O God, like your name,
   reaches the ends of the earth.

   Your right hand is filled with saving justice.
¹² Mount Sion rejoices.
   The daughters of Judah rejoice
   at the sight of your judgments.

¹³ Walk through Sion, walk all around her;
   count the number of her towers.
¹⁴ Consider all her ramparts;
   examine her castles,

   That you may tell the next generation
¹⁵ that such is our God,
   our God forever and always.
   He will guide us forever.

Psalm 49 (48)

¹ *For the Choirmaster. Of the sons of Korah. A Psalm.*

² Hear this, all you peoples,
   give ear, all who dwell in the world,
³ people both high and low,
   rich and poor alike!

⁴ My mouth will utter wisdom.
   The reflections of my heart offer insight.
⁵ I will incline my ear to a mystery;
   with the harp I will set forth my problem.

⁶ Why should I fear in evil days
   the malice of the foes who surround me,
⁷ those who trust in their wealth,
   and boast of the vastness of their riches?

⁸ No man can ransom a brother,
   nor pay a price to God for his life.
⁹ How high is the price of his soul!
   The ransom can never be enough!
¹⁰ No one can buy life unending,
   nor avoid coming to the grave.

¹¹ Anyone sees that the wise will die;
   the foolish will perish with the senseless,
   and leave their wealth to others.

¹² Their graves are their homes forever,
    their dwelling place from age to age,
    though lands were called by their names.

¹³ In his riches, man does not endure;
    he is like the beasts that are destroyed.

¹⁴ This is the way of the foolish,
    the outcome of those pleased with their lot:
¹⁵ like sheep they are driven to the grave,
    where death shall become their shepherd,
    and the upright shall have dominion.

    Their outward show wastes away with the morning,
    and the grave becomes their home.
¹⁶ But God will ransom my soul from the grasp of
        hell;
    for he indeed will receive me.

¹⁷ Then do not fear when a man grows rich,
    when the glory of his house increases.
¹⁸ He takes nothing with him when he dies;
    his glory does not follow him below.

¹⁹ Though he flattered himself while he lived,
    "People will praise me for all my success,"
²⁰ yet he will go to join his forebears,
    and will never see the light anymore.

²¹ In his riches, man cannot discern;
    he is like the beasts that are destroyed.

Psalm 50 *(49)*

¹ *A Psalm of Asaph.*

> The God of gods, the LORD,
> has spoken and summoned the earth,
> from the rising of the sun to its setting.
> ² Out of Sion, the perfection of beauty,
> God is shining forth.

³ Our God comes, and does not keep silence.
Before him fire devours;
around him tempest rages.
⁴ He calls on the heavens above,
and on the earth, to judge his people.

⁵ "Gather my holy ones to me,
who made covenant with me by sacrifice."
⁶ The heavens proclaim his justice,
for he, God, is the judge.

⁷ "Listen, my people, I will speak;
Israel, I will testify against you,
for I am God, your God.

⁸ I do not rebuke you for your sacrifices;
your offerings are always before me.
⁹ I do not take more bullocks from your farms,
nor goats from among your herds.

¹⁰ For I own all the beasts of the forest,
beasts in their thousands on my hills.
¹¹ I know all the birds on the mountains;
all that moves in the field belongs to me.

¹² Were I hungry, I would not tell you,
    for the world and its fullness is mine.
¹³ Do I eat the flesh of bulls,
    or drink the blood of goats?

¹⁴ Give your praise as a sacrifice to God,
    and fulfill your vows to the Most High.
¹⁵ Then call on me in the day of distress.
    I will deliver you and you shall honor me."

¹⁶ But God will say to the wicked,
    "How can you recite my commandments,
    and take my covenant on your lips,
¹⁷ you who despise correction,
    and cast my words behind you,

¹⁸ You who see a thief and befriend him,
    who throw in your lot with adulterers,
¹⁹ who unbridle your mouth for evil,
    and yoke your tongue to deceit,
²⁰ you who sit and malign your own brother,
    and slander your own mother's son?

²¹ You do this, and should I keep silence?
    Do you think that I am like you?
    I accuse you, lay the charge before you.

²² Mark this, you who are forgetful of God,
    lest I seize you and none can deliver you.
²³ A sacrifice of praise gives me honor,
    and to one whose way is blameless,
    I will show the salvation of God."

Psalm 51 (50)

¹ *For the Choirmaster. A Psalm of David* ² *when the*
prophet Nathan came to him after he had gone to
Bathsheba.

³ Have mercy on me, O God,
according to your merciful love;
according to your great compassion,
blot out my transgressions.
⁴ Wash me completely from my iniquity,
and cleanse me from my sin.

⁵ My transgressions, truly I know them;
my sin is always before me.
⁶ Against you, you alone, have I sinned;
what is evil in your sight I have done.
So you are just in your sentence,
without reproach in your judgment.

⁷ O see, in guilt I was born,
a sinner when my mother conceived me.
⁸ Yes, you delight in sincerity of heart;
in secret you teach me wisdom.
⁹ Cleanse me with hyssop, and I shall be pure;
wash me, and I shall be whiter than snow.

¹⁰ Let me hear rejoicing and gladness,
that the bones you have crushed may exult.
¹¹ Turn away your face from my sins,
and blot out all my guilt.

¹² Create a pure heart for me, O God;
    renew a steadfast spirit within me.
¹³ Do not cast me away from your presence;
    take not your holy spirit from me.

¹⁴ Restore in me the joy of your salvation;
    sustain in me a willing spirit.
¹⁵ I will teach transgressors your ways,
    that sinners may return to you.

¹⁶ Rescue me from bloodshed, O God,
    God of my salvation,
    and then my tongue shall ring out your justice.
¹⁷ O Lord, open my lips
    and my mouth shall proclaim your praise.

¹⁸ For in sacrifice you take no delight;
    burnt offering from me would not please you.
¹⁹ My sacrifice to God, a broken spirit:
    a broken and humbled heart,
    O God, you will not spurn.

²⁰ In your good pleasure, show favor to Sion;
    rebuild the walls of Jerusalem.
²¹ Then you will delight in right sacrifice,
    burnt offerings wholly consumed.
    Then you will be offered young bulls on your altar.

Psalm 52 (51)

1 *For the Choirmaster. A* Maskil *of David* 2 *after*
Doeg the Edomite came and told Saul, "David
has gone to the house of Abimelech."

3 Why do you boast of wickedness,
you champion of evil?
4 Planning ruin all day long,
your tongue is like a sharpened razor,
you who practice deceit!

5 You love evil more than good,
falsehood more than truth.
6 You love every destructive word,
O tongue of deceit.

7 Then God will break you down forever,
and he will take you away.
He will snatch you from your tent, and uproot you
from the land of the living.

8 The just shall see and fear.
  They shall laugh and say,
9 "So this is the champion who refused
  to take God as a stronghold,
  but trusted in the greatness of wealth
  and grew powerful by wickedness."

10 But I am like a growing olive tree
  in the house of God.
  I trust in the mercy of God,
  forever and ever.

11 I will thank you forevermore,
  for this is your doing.
  I will hope in your name, for it is good,
  in the presence of your faithful.

Psalm 53 *(52)*

¹ *For the Choirmaster. Intoned like* Mahalat.
   A Maskil *of David.*

² The fool has said in his heart,
   "There is no God."
   Their deeds are corrupt, depraved;
   no one does any good.

³ God looks down from heaven
   on the human race,
   to see if any are wise,
   if any seek God.

⁴ All have left the right path,
   depraved, every one;
   there is no one who does any good,
   no, not even one.

5 Do none who do evil understand?
  They eat up my people as if eating bread;
  they never call out to God.

6 There they shall tremble with fear—
  without cause for fear—
  for God scatters the bones of your besiegers.
  They are shamed; God rejects them.

7 Who will bring Israel salvation from Sion?
  When God brings about the return of his people,
  then Jacob will be glad and Israel rejoice.

Psalm 54 *(53)*

¹ *For the Choirmaster. On stringed instruments. A Maskil of David* ² *after the Ziphites came to Saul and said, "Is not David hiding among us?"*

³ O God, save me by your name;
   by your power, defend my cause.
⁴ O God, hear my prayer;
   give ear to the words of my mouth.

⁵ For the proud have risen against me,
   and the ruthless seek my life.
   They have no regard for God.

⁶ See, I have God for my help.
   The Lord sustains my soul.
⁷ Let evil recoil on my foes.
   In your faithfulness, bring them to an end.

⁸ I will sacrifice to you with willing heart,
   and praise your name, for it is good:
⁹ for it has rescued me from all distress,
   and my eyes have gazed upon my foes.

Psalm 55 (54)

¹ *For the Choirmaster. On stringed instruments.
A* Maskil *of David.*

² Give ear, O God, to my prayer;
  do not hide from my pleading.
³ Attend to me and reply;
  with my cares, I cannot rest.

⁴ I tremble at the shouts of the foe,
  at the cries of the wicked,
  for they pile up evil upon me;
  in anger they malign me.

⁵ My heart is stricken within me;
  death's terror falls upon me.
⁶ Trembling and fear come over me,
  and horror overwhelms me.

⁷ I say, "O that I had wings like a dove,
  to fly away and be at rest!
⁸ I would indeed escape far away,
  and take refuge in the desert.
⁹ I shall await him who saves me
  from the raging wind and tempest."

¹⁰ Engulf and confuse their speech, O Lord,
  for I see violence and strife in the city!
¹¹ Night and day they patrol its walls.
  In its midst are wickedness and evil.

¹² Destruction lies within it.
  Its streets are never free
  from tyranny and deceit.

¹³ If an enemy made taunts against me,
  I could bear it.
  If my rival had risen against me,
  I could hide from him.

¹⁴ But it is you, as my equal, my friend,
  whom I knew so well,
¹⁵ with whom I enjoyed friendly counsel!
  We walked together in harmony
  in the house of God.

¹⁶ May death fall suddenly upon them!
  Let them go down alive to the grave,
  for wickedness dwells in their homes,
  and deep in their hearts.

¹⁷ As for me, I will cry to God,
  and the LORD will save me.
¹⁸ Evening, morning, and at noon,
  I will cry and lament,
  and he will hear my voice.

¹⁹ He will redeem my soul in peace
  in the attack against me,
  for those who fight me are many.

²⁰ God, who is enthroned forever,
  will hear them and humble them.
  For they will not amend their ways;
  they have no fear of God.

²¹ The traitor has turned against his friends;
  he has broken his pact.
²² His speech is softer than butter,
  but war is in his heart.
  His words are smoother than oil,
  but they are swords unsheathed.

²³ Entrust your cares to the LORD,
  and he will support you.
  He will never allow
  the just man to stumble.

²⁴ But you will bring them down, O God,
  to the pit of death:
  the bloodthirsty and the liars
  shall not live even half their days.
  But I, I will trust in you, O Lord.

Psalm 56 (55)

¹ *For the Choirmaster. Intoned like "The Dove of
Distant Places." A* Miktam *of David, when the
Philistines seized him in Gath.*

² Have mercy on me, O God,
for people assail me;
they fight me all day long and oppress me.
³ My foes assail me all day long:
many fight proudly against me.

⁴ On the day when I shall fear,
I will trust in you,
⁵ in God, whose word I praise.
In God I trust; I shall not fear.
What can mere flesh do to me?

⁶ All day long they distort my words;
their every thought against me is evil.
⁷ They band together in ambush;
they watch my very footsteps,
as they wait to take my life.

⁸ Repay them, O God, for their crimes;
   in your anger, bring down the peoples.
⁹ You have kept an account of my wanderings;
   you have placed my tears in your flask;
   are they not recorded in your book?
¹⁰ Then my foes will turn back
   on the day when I call to you.

   This I know, that God is on my side.
¹¹ In God, whose word I praise,
   in the LORD whose word I praise,
¹² in God I trust; I shall not fear.
   What can man do to me?

¹³ I am bound by the vows I have made you.
   O God, I will offer you praise,
¹⁴ for you have rescued my soul from death;
   you kept my feet from stumbling,
   that I may walk in the presence of God,
   in the light of the living.

Psalm 57 (56)

¹ *For the Choirmaster. Intoned like "Do not destroy."*
A Miktam *of David when he fled from Saul into*
a cave.

² Have mercy on me, God, have mercy,
  for in you my soul has taken refuge.
  In the shadow of your wings I take refuge,
  till the storms of destruction pass by.

³ I call to you, God the Most High,
  to God who provides for me.
⁴ May he send from heaven and save me,
  and put to shame those who assail me.
  May God send his loving mercy and faithfulness.

⁵ My soul lies down among lions,
  who would devour the sons of men.
  Their teeth are spears and arrows,
  their tongue a sharpened sword.
⁶ Be exalted, O God, above the heavens;
  may your glory shine on earth!

⁷ They laid down a net for my steps;
  my soul was bowed down.
  They dug a pit in my path,
  but fell in it themselves.

⁸ My heart is ready, O God;
  my heart is ready.
  I will sing, I will sing your praise.
⁹ Awake, my soul!
  Awake, lyre and harp!
  I will awake the dawn.

¹⁰ I will praise you, Lord, among the peoples,
  among the nations sing psalms to you,
¹¹ for your mercy reaches to the heavens,
  and your truth to the skies.
¹² Be exalted, O God, above the heavens;
  may your glory shine on all the earth!

Psalm 58 *(57)*

¹ *For the Choirmaster. Intoned like "Do not destroy."*
A Miktam *of David.*

² Do you truly speak justice, you who hold divine
power?
Do you mete out fair judgment to the sons of men?
³ No, in your hearts you devise iniquities;
your hands deal out violence to the land.

⁴ The wicked go astray from the womb;
deviant from birth, they speak lies.
⁵ Their venom is like the venom of the snake;
they are like a deaf viper stopping its ears,
⁶ lest it should hear the snake-charmer's voice,
the voice of the skillful dealer in spells.

⁷ O God, break the teeth in their mouths;
  tear out the fangs of these lions, O LORD!
⁸ Let them vanish like water that runs away;
  let them wither like grass that is trodden underfoot.
⁹ Let them be like the snail that dissolves into slime,
  like a woman's miscarriage that never sees the sun.

¹⁰ Before they put forth thorns, like a bramble,
  let them be swept away, green wood or dry!
¹¹ The just shall rejoice at the sight of vengeance;
  they shall bathe their feet in the blood of the
        wicked.
¹² People shall say: "Truly, there is reward for the
        upright.
  Truly there is a God who judges justly on earth."

Psalm 59 *(58)*

¹ *For the Choirmaster. Intoned like "Do not destroy."*
A Miktam of David when Saul sent men to keep
watch on his house and kill him.

² Rescue me from my foes, O God;
  protect me from those who attack me.
³ O rescue me from those who do evil,
  and save me from bloodthirsty men.

⁴ See, they lie in wait for my life;
  the strong band together against me.
  For no offense, no sin of mine, O LORD,
⁵ for no guilt of mine they rush to take their stand.

  Awake! Come to meet me, and see!
⁶ LORD God of hosts, you are Israel's God.
  Rouse yourself and punish the nations;
  show no mercy to evil traitors.
⁷ Each evening they come back;
  howling like dogs, they roam about the city.

⁸ See how their mouths utter insults;
  their lips are like sharpened swords.
  "For who," they say, "will hear us?"
⁹ But you, LORD, will laugh them to scorn.
  You make a mockery of all the nations.

¹⁰ O my Strength, for you will I watch,
  for you, O God, are my stronghold,
¹¹ the God who shows me merciful love.

Now God will proceed before me;
God will let me look upon my foes.
¹² Do not kill them lest my people forget;
rout them by your power, lay them low.

It is you, Lord God, who are our shield.
¹³ For the sins of their mouths and the words of
their lips,
let them be caught in their pride;
for the curses and lies that they speak.

¹⁴ Destroy them in your anger. Destroy them
till they are no more.
Let them know that God is the ruler
over Jacob and the ends of the earth.

¹⁵ Each evening they come back;
they howl like dogs and roam about the city.
¹⁶ They prowl in search of food;
they growl till they have their fill.

¹⁷ As for me, I will sing of your strength,
and acclaim your mercy in the morning,
for you have been my stronghold,
a refuge in the day of my distress.

¹⁸ O my Strength, to you I will sing praise,
for you, O God, are my stronghold,
the God who shows me merciful love.

Psalm 60 (59)

¹ *For the Choirmaster. Intoned like "The Lily of*
  Testimony." A Miktam *of David for instruction*
  when he went out against the Aram-Haharaim
  and Aram-Sobah, and when Joab returned to
  Edom and defeated twelve thousand in the Valley
  of Salt.

³ O God, you have rejected us, and broken us.
  You have been angry; come back to us.

⁴ You have made the earth quake, torn it open.
  Repair what is shattered, for it sways.
⁵ You have inflicted hardships on your people,
  made us drink a wine that dazed us.

⁶ For those who fear you, you gave the signal
  to flee from the face of the bow.
⁷ With your right hand, grant salvation, and give
            answer,
  that those whom you love may be free.

⁸ From his holy place God has spoken:
  "I will exult, and divide the land of Shechem;
  I will measure out the valley of Succoth.

⁹ Mine is Gilead, mine is Manasseh;
  Ephraim I take for my helmet,
  Judah is my scepter.

¹⁰ Moab is my washbowl;
  on Edom I will cast my shoe.
  Over Philistia I will shout in triumph."

¹¹ But who will lead me to the fortified city?
  Who will bring me to Edom?
¹² Have you, O God, rejected us?
  Will you march with our armies no longer?

¹³ Give us help against the foe,
  for the help of man is vain.
¹⁴ With God, we shall do bravely,
  and he will trample down our foes.

Psalm 61 (60)

¹ *For the Choirmaster. With stringed instruments.*
   Of David.

² Listen, O God, to my cry!
   Attend to my prayer!
³ From the end of the earth I call you;
   my heart is faint.

   Set me high upon the rock
   too high for me to reach,
⁴ you, my refuge and mighty tower
   against the foe.

⁵ Then will I dwell in your tent forever,
   and hide in the shelter of your wings.
⁶ For you, O God, have heard my vows;
   you have given me the heritage of those
   who fear your name.

⁷ Day upon day you will add to the king;
   his years as age upon age.
⁸ May he ever sit enthroned before God:
   bid mercy and truth be his protection.
⁹ So I will sing to your name forever,
   and day after day fulfill my vows.

Psalm 62 (61)

[1] *For the Choirmaster. Intoned like Jeduthun. A Psalm of David.*

[2] In God alone is my soul at rest;
   my salvation comes from him.
[3] He alone is my rock, my salvation,
   my fortress; never shall I falter.

[4] How long will you all attack one man
   to break him down,
   as though he were a tottering wall,
   or a tumbling fence?

[5] Their plan is only to bring down;
   they take pleasure in lies.
   With their mouth they utter blessing,
   but in their heart they curse.

[6] In God alone be at rest, my soul,
   for my hope is from him.
[7] He alone is my rock, my salvation,
   my fortress; never shall I falter.

⁸ In God is my salvation and glory,
  my rock of strength;
  in God is my refuge.
⁹ Trust him at all times, O people.
  Pour out your hearts before him,
  for God is our refuge.

¹⁰ The sons of men are a breath,
  an illusion, the sons of men.
  Placed in the scales, they rise;
  they all weigh less than a breath.

¹¹ Do not put your trust in oppression,
  nor vain hopes on plunder.
  Even if riches increase,
  set not your heart on them.

¹² For God has said only one thing;
  only two have I heard:
  that to God alone belongs power,
¹³ and to you, Lord, merciful love;
  and that you repay each man
  according to his deeds.

Psalm 63 *(62)*

¹ *A Psalm of David when he was in the desert of Judah.*

² O God, you are my God; at dawn I seek you;
   for you my soul is thirsting.
   For you my flesh is pining,
   like a dry, weary land without water.
³ I have come before you in the sanctuary,
   to behold your strength and your glory.

⁴ Your loving mercy is better than life;
   my lips will speak your praise.
⁵ I will bless you all my life;
   in your name I will lift up my hands.
⁶ My soul shall be filled as with a banquet;
   with joyful lips, my mouth shall praise you.

⁷ When I remember you upon my bed,
  I muse on you through the watches of the night.
⁸ For you have been my strength;
  in the shadow of your wings I rejoice.
⁹ My soul clings fast to you;
  your right hand upholds me.

¹⁰ Those who seek to destroy my life
  shall go down to the depths of the earth.
¹¹ Put to the power of the sword,
  they shall be left as prey for the jackals.

¹² But the king shall rejoice in God;
  all that swear by him shall exult,
  for the mouth of liars shall be silenced.

Psalm 64 (63)

For the Choirmaster. A Psalm of David.

2 Hear, O God, the voice of my complaint;
  guard my life from dread of the foe.
3 From the assembly of the wicked, hide me,
  from the throng of those who do evil.

4 They sharpen their tongues like swords.
  They aim bitter words like arrows,
5 to shoot at the innocent from ambush,
  shooting suddenly and fearlessly.

6 Holding firm in their evil course,
  they conspire to lay secret snares.
  They say, "Who will see us?
7 Who can search out our crimes?"

They have hatched their wicked plots,
and brought them to perfection.
How profound the depths of the heart!

8 God will shoot them with his arrow,
and deal them sudden wounds.
9 Their own tongue brings them to ruin;
all who see them shake their heads.

10 Then will all be afraid;
they will tell what God has done.
They will ponder God's deeds.
11 The just one will rejoice in the LORD;
and fly to him for refuge.
All upright hearts will glory.

Psalm 65 (64)

¹ *For the Choirmaster. A Psalm of David. A Song.*

² Praise is due to you
  in Sion, O God.
  To you we pay our vows in Jerusalem,
³ you who hear our prayer.

  To you all flesh will come.
⁴ Our evil deeds are too heavy for us,
  but our transgressions you wipe away.

⁵ Blessed is he whom you choose and call
  to dwell in your courts.
  We are filled with the good things of your house,
  of your holy temple.

⁶ With wondrous deliverance you answer us,
  O God our savior.
  You are the hope of all the earth,
  and of far distant isles.

⁷ You establish the mountains with your strength;
  you are girded with power.
⁸ You still the roaring of the seas,
  the roaring of their waves,
  and the tumult of the peoples.

⁹ Distant peoples stand in awe
    at your wondrous deeds.
    The lands of sunrise and sunset
    you fill with your joy.

¹⁰ You visit the earth, give it water;
    you fill it with riches.
    God's ever-flowing river brims over
    to prepare the grain.

    And thus you provide for the earth:
¹¹ you drench its furrows;
    you level it, soften it with showers;
    you bless its growth.

¹² You crown the year with your bounty.
    Abundance flows in your pathways;
¹³ in pastures of the desert it flows.

    The hills are girded with joy,
¹⁴ the meadows clothed with flocks.
    The valleys are decked with wheat.
    They shout for joy; yes, they sing!

Psalm 66 (65)

¹ *For the Choirmaster. A Song. A Psalm.*

Cry out with joy to God, all the earth;
² O sing to the glory of his name.
O render him glorious praise.
³ Say to God, "How awesome your deeds!

Because of the greatness of your strength,
your enemies fawn upon you.
⁴ Before you all the earth shall bow down,
shall sing to you, sing to your name!"

⁵ Come and see the works of God:
awesome his deeds among the children of men.
⁶ He turned the sea into dry land;
they passed through the river on foot.

Let our joy, then, be in him;
⁷ he rules forever by his might.
His eyes keep watch on the nations:
let rebels not exalt themselves.

⁸ O peoples, bless our God;
let the voice of his praise resound,
⁹ of the God who gave life to our souls
and kept our feet from stumbling.

¹⁰ For you, O God, have tested us,
  you have tried us as silver is tried;
¹¹ you led us, God, into the snare;
  you laid a heavy burden on our backs.

¹² You let men ride over our heads;
  we went through fire and through water,
  but then you brought us to a place of plenty.

¹³ Burnt offering I bring to your house;
  to you I will pay my vows,
¹⁴ the vows which my lips have uttered,
  which my mouth declared in my distress.

¹⁵ I will offer you burnt offerings of fatlings
  with the smoke of sacrificial rams.
  I will offer bullocks and goats.

¹⁶ Come and hear, all who fear God;
  I will tell what he did for my soul.
¹⁷ To him I cried aloud,
  with exaltation ready on my tongue.

¹⁸ Had I considered evil in my heart,
  the Lord would not have listened.
¹⁹ But truly God has listened;
  he has heeded the voice of my prayer.
²⁰ Blest be God, who did not reject my prayer,
  nor withhold from me his merciful love.

Psalm 67 (66)

*¹ For the Choirmaster. With string instruments.
A Psalm. A Song.*

² O God, be gracious and bless us
and let your face shed its light upon us.
³ So will your ways be known upon earth
and all nations learn your salvation.

⁴ Let the peoples praise you, O God;
let all the peoples praise you.

⁵ Let the nations be glad and shout for joy,
with uprightness you rule the peoples;
you guide the nations on earth.

⁶ Let the peoples praise you, O God;
let all the peoples praise you.

⁷ The earth has yielded its fruit
for God, our God, has blessed us.
⁸ May God still give us his blessing
that all the ends of the earth may revere him.

Psalm 68 (67)

¹ *For the Choirmaster. Of David. A Psalm. A Song.*

² Let God arise; let his foes be scattered.
Let those who hate him flee from his presence.
³ As smoke is driven away, so drive them away;
like wax that melts before the fire,
so the wicked shall perish at the presence of God.

⁴ But the just shall rejoice at the presence of God;
they shall exult with glad rejoicing.
⁵ O sing to God; make music to his name.
Extol the One who rides on the clouds.
The LORD is his name; exult at his presence.

⁶ Father of orphans, defender of widows:
such is God in his holy place.
⁷ God gives the desolate a home to dwell in;
he leads the prisoners forth into prosperity,
but rebels must dwell in a parched land.

⁸ O God, when you went forth before your people,
when you marched out across the desert,
⁹ the earth trembled, heavens poured down rain:
at the face of God, the God of Sinai,
at the face of God, the God of Israel.

¹⁰ You poured down, O God, a generous rain;
   when your people languished, you restored their
      inheritance.
¹¹ It was there that your flock began to dwell.
   In your goodness, O God, you provided for the
      poor.

¹² The Lord announces the command;
   a mighty throng bears good tidings:
¹³ "The kings and armies are in headlong flight,
   while you were at rest among the sheepfolds."

¹⁴ At home the women already share the spoil.
   They are covered with silver as the wings of a
      dove,
   its feathers brilliant with shining gold.
¹⁵ When the Almighty scatters kings on the
      mountain,
   it is like snow whitening Mount Zalmon.

¹⁶ You, mountain of Bashan, are a mighty
      mountain;
   a many-peaked mountain, the mountain of
      Bashan.
¹⁷ Why look with envy, you many-peaked
      mountain,
   at the mountain where God has desired to dwell?
   It is there that the Lord shall dwell forever.

¹⁸ The chariots of God are thousands upon thousands.
  The Lord has come from Sinai to the holy place.
¹⁹ You have ascended on high; leading captivity
        captive
  as tribute receiving prisoners, O God,
  so that even rebels may dwell near the LORD God.

²⁰ Day after day, may the Lord be blest.
  He bears our burdens; God is our savior.
²¹ This God of ours is a God who saves.
  The LORD our Lord provides an escape from
        death.
²² And God will smite the head of his foes,
  the hairy crown of him who walks about in his
        guilt.

²³ The Lord said, "I will bring them back from
        Bashan;
  I will bring them back from the depth of the sea.
²⁴ Then you will bathe your feet in their blood,
  and the tongues of your dogs take their share of
        the foe."

²⁵ They see your solemn procession, O God,
  the procession of my God, of my king, to the holy
        place:
²⁶ the singers in the forefront, the musicians coming
        last;
  between them, maidens sounding their timbrels.

27 "In the sacred assembly, bless God, the LORD,
   O you who are from the fountain of Israel."
28 There is Benjamin, least of the tribes, at the head;
   Judah's princes, a mighty throng;
   Zebulun's princes, Naphtali's princes.

29 Summon forth your might, O God;
   your might, O God, which you have shown for us.
30 From your temple high in Jerusalem,
   kings will come to you bringing their tribute.

31 Rebuke the wild beast that dwells in the reeds,
   the bands of the mighty and rulers of the peoples.
   Scatter the peoples who delight in war.
32 Rich merchants will make their way from Egypt;
   Ethiopia will stretch out her hands to God.

33 You kingdoms of the earth, sing to God, praise
         the Lord
34 who rides on the heavens, the ancient heavens.
   Behold, he thunders his voice, his mighty voice.
35 Come, acknowledge the power of God.

   His glory is on Israel; his might is in the skies.
36 Awesome is God in his holy place.
   He is God, the God of Israel.
   He himself gives strength and power to his people.
   Blest be God!

Psalm 69 *(68)*

¹ *For the Choirmaster. Intoned like "Lilies."*
   Of David.

² Save me, O God, for the waters
   have risen to my neck.
³ I have sunk into the mud of the deep,
   where there is no foothold.
   I have entered the waters of the deep,
   where the flood overwhelms me.

⁴ I am wearied with crying aloud;
   my throat is parched.
   My eyes are wasted away
   with waiting for my God.

⁵ More numerous than the hairs on my head
   are those who hate me without cause.
   Many are those who attack me,
   enemies with lies.
   What I have never stolen,
   how can I restore?

⁶ O God, you know my folly;
   from you my sins are not hidden.
⁷ May those who hope in you not be shamed
   because of me, O Lord of hosts;
   may those who seek you not be put to shame
   because of me, O God of Israel.

8 It is for you that I suffer taunts,
   that shame has covered my face.
9 To my own kin I have become an outcast,
   a stranger to the children of my mother.
10 Zeal for your house consumes me,
   and taunts against you fall on me.

11 When my soul wept bitterly in fasting,
   they made it a taunt against me.
12 When I made my clothing sackcloth,
   I became a reproach to them,
13 the gossip of those at the gates,
   the theme of drunkards' songs.

14 But I pray to you, O LORD,
   for a time of your favor.
   In your great mercy, answer me, O God,
   with your salvation that never fails.

15 Rescue me from sinking in the mud;
   from those who hate me, deliver me.
   Save me from the waters of the deep,
16 lest the waves overwhelm me.
   Let not the deep engulf me,
   nor the pit close its mouth on me.

¹⁷ LORD, answer, for your mercy is kind;
in your great compassion, turn toward me.
¹⁸ Do not hide your face from your servant;
answer me quickly, for I am in distress.
¹⁹ Come close to my soul and redeem me;
ransom me because of my foes.

²⁰ You know my taunts, my shame, my dishonor;
my oppressors are all before you.
²¹ Taunts have broken my heart;
here I am in anguish.
I looked for solace, but there was none;
for consolers—not one could I find.

²² For food they gave me gall;
in my thirst they gave me vinegar to drink.
²³ Let their table be a snare to them,
and for their friends, a trap.
²⁴ Let their eyes grow dim and blind;
let their limbs continually tremble.

²⁵ Pour out your anger upon them;
let your burning fury overtake them.
²⁶ Let their camp be left desolate;
let no one dwell in their tents:
²⁷ for they persecute one whom you struck;
they increase the pain of one whom you wounded.

²⁸ Charge them with guilt upon guilt;
    let them have no share in your justice.
²⁹ Blot them out from the book of the living;
    do not enroll them among the just.
³⁰ As for me in my poverty and pain,
    let your salvation, O God, raise me up.

³¹ Then I will praise God's name with a song;
    I will glorify him with thanksgiving:
³² a gift pleasing God more than oxen,
    more than a bull with horns and hoofs.

³³ The poor when they see it will be glad,
    and God-seeking hearts will revive;
³⁴ for the LORD listens to the needy,
    and does not spurn his own in their chains.
³⁵ Let the heavens and the earth give him praise,
    the seas and everything that moves in them.

³⁶ For God will bring salvation to Sion,
    and rebuild the cities of Judah,
    and they shall dwell there in possession.
³⁷ The children of his servants shall inherit it;
    those who love his name shall dwell there.

Psalm 70 (69)

¹ *For the Choirmaster. Of David. A Memorial.*

² O God, come to my assistance;
  O LORD, make haste to help me!
³ Let there be shame and confusion
  on those who seek my life.

  O let them turn back in confusion,
  who delight in my harm;
⁴ let them retreat, covered with shame,
  who jeer at me and mock.

⁵ O let there be rejoicing and gladness
  for all who seek you.
  Let them say forever, "God is great,"
  who love your saving help.

⁶ As for me, wretched and poor,
  hasten to me, O God.
  You are my rescuer, my help;
  O LORD, do not delay.

Psalm 71 (70)

¹ In you, O LORD, I take refuge;
   let me never be put to shame.
² In your justice, rescue me, free me;
   incline your ear to me and save me.

³ Be my rock, my constant refuge,
   a mighty stronghold to save me,
   for you are my rock, my stronghold.
⁴ My God, free me from the hand of the wicked,
   from the grip of the unjust, of the oppressor.

⁵ It is you, O Lord, who are my hope,
   my trust, O LORD, from my youth.
⁶ On you I have leaned from my birth;
   from my mother's womb, you have been my help.
   At all times I give you praise.

⁷ My fate has filled many with awe,
   but you are my mighty refuge.
⁸ My mouth is filled with your praise,
   with your glory, all the day long.
⁹ Do not reject me now that I am old;
   when my strength fails do not forsake me.

¹⁰ For my enemies are speaking about me;
    those who watch me take counsel together,
¹¹ saying: "God has forsaken him; follow him.
    Seize him; there is no one to save him."
¹² O God, do not stay afar off;
    O my God, make haste to help me!

¹³ Let them be put to shame and destroyed,
    those who seek my life.
    Let them be covered with shame and confusion,
    those who seek to harm me.

¹⁴ But as for me, I will always hope,
    and praise you more and more.
¹⁵ My mouth will tell of your justice,
    and all the day long of your salvation,
    though I can never tell it all.

¹⁶ I will come with praise of your might, O Lord;
    I will call to mind your justice,
    yours, O Lord, alone.
¹⁷ O God, you have taught me from my youth,
    and I proclaim your wonders still.

¹⁸ Even till I am old and gray-headed,
   do not forsake me, O God.
   Let me tell of your mighty arm
   to every coming generation;
¹⁹ your strength and your justice, O God,
   reach to the highest heavens.
   It is you who have worked such wonders.
   O God, who is like you?

²⁰ You have made me witness many troubles and
         evils,
   but you will give me back my life.
   You will raise me from the depths of the earth;
²¹ you will exalt me and console me again.

²² So I will give you thanks on the lyre
   for your faithfulness, O my God.
   To you will I sing with the harp,
   to you, the Holy One of Israel.
²³ When I sing to you, my lips shall shout for joy,
   and my soul, which you have redeemed.

²⁴ And all the day long my tongue
   shall tell the tale of your justice,
   for they are put to shame and disgraced,
   those who seek to harm me.

Psalm 72 (71)

¹ *Of Solomon.*

O God, give your judgment to the king,
to a king's son your justice,
² that he may judge your people in justice,
and your poor in right judgment.

³ May the mountains bring forth peace for the people,
and the hills justice.
⁴ May he defend the poor of the people,
and save the children of the needy,
and crush the oppressor.

⁵ He shall endure like the sun and the moon
through all generations.
⁶ He shall descend like rain on the meadow,
like showers that water the earth.
⁷ In his days shall justice flourish,
and great peace till the moon is no more.

⁸ He shall rule from sea to sea,
from the River to the bounds of the earth.
⁹ Let the desert dwellers fall before him,
and his enemies lick the dust.

¹⁰ The kings of Tarshish and the islands
  shall pay him tribute.
  The kings of Sheba and Seba
  shall bring him gifts.
¹¹ Before him all kings shall fall prostrate,
  all nations shall serve him.

¹² For he shall save the needy when they cry,
  the poor, and those who are helpless.
¹³ He will have pity on the weak and the needy,
  and save the lives of the needy.
¹⁴ From oppression and violence he redeems their
      souls;
  to him their blood is dear.

¹⁵ Long may he live!
  May the gold of Sheba be given him.
  They shall pray for him without ceasing,
  and bless him all the day.

¹⁶ May grain be abundant in the land,
  waving to the peaks of the mountains.
  May its fruit rustle like Lebanon;
  may the people flourish in the cities
  like grass on the earth.

[17] May his name endure forever,
his name continue like the sun.
Every tribe shall be blest in him,
all nations shall call him blessed.

*   *   *

[18] Blest be the LORD, God of Israel,
who alone works wonders,
[19] ever blest his glorious name.
Let his glory fill the earth.
Amen! Amen!

[20] Here end the Psalms of David, son of Jesse.

BOOK THREE
Of The Psalter

Psalm 73 (72)

A Psalm of Asaph.

How good is God to Israel,
to those who are pure of heart!
² As for me, I came close to stumbling;
my feet had almost slipped,
³ for I was filled with envy of the proud,
when I saw how the wicked prosper.

⁴ For them there are no pains;
their bodies are sound and sleek.
⁵ They do not share in people's burdens;
they are not stricken like others.

⁶ So they wear their pride like a necklace;
they clothe themselves with violence.
⁷ With folds of fat, their eyes protrude.
With imagination their hearts overflow.

⁸ They scoff; they speak with malice.
From on high they threaten oppression.
⁹ They have set their mouths in the heavens,
and their tongues are roaming the earth.

¹⁰ So the people turn to them
and drink in all their words.
¹¹ They say, "How can God know?
Does the Most High have any knowledge?"
¹² Look at them, such are the wicked;
ever prosperous, they grow in wealth.

¹³ How useless to keep my heart pure,
and wash my hands in innocence,
¹⁴ when I was stricken all day long,
suffered punishment with each new morning.
¹⁵ Then I said, "If I should speak like that,
I should betray your children's generation."

¹⁶ I strove to fathom this problem,
too hard for my mind to understand,
¹⁷ until I entered the holy place of God,
and came to discern their end.

¹⁸ How slippery the paths on which you set them;
you make them fall to destruction.
¹⁹ How suddenly they come to their ruin,
swept away, destroyed by terrors.
²⁰ Like a dream one wakes from, O Lord,
when you wake you dismiss them as phantoms.

²¹ And so when my heart grew embittered,
   and I was pierced to the depths of my being,
²² I was stupid and did not understand;
   I was like a beast in your sight.

²³ As for me, I was always in your presence;
   you were holding me by my right hand.
²⁴ By your counsel you will guide me,
   and then you will lead me to glory.

²⁵ What else have I in heaven but you?
   Apart from you, I want nothing on earth.
²⁶ My body and my heart waste away;
   God is the strength of my heart;
   God is my portion forever.

²⁷ Surely, those who are far from you perish;
   you destroy all those who are unfaithful.
²⁸ To be near God is my happiness;
   I have my hope in the Lord God.
   I will proclaim your works
   at the gates of daughter Sion.

Psalm 74 *(73)*

¹ *A Maskil* of *Asaph.*

Why, O God, have you cast us off forever?
Why does your anger blaze at the sheep of your
      pasture?
² Remember your flock which you claimed long
      ago,
the tribe you redeemed to be your own possession,
this mountain of Sion where you made your
      dwelling.

³ Turn your steps to these places that are utterly
      ruined!
The enemy has laid waste the whole of the holy
      place.
⁴ Your foes have made uproar in the midst of your
      assembly;
they have set up their emblems as tokens there.
⁵ They have wielded their axes on high,
as at the entrance to a grove of trees.

⁶ They have broken down all the carvings;
they have struck together with hatchet and pickax.
⁷ O God, they have set your holy place on fire;
they have razed and profaned the abode of your
      name.

⁸ They said in their hearts, "We will utterly crush
>   them;
>   we will burn every shrine of God in the land."
⁹ We do not see our emblems, nor is there a
>   prophet;
>   we have no one to tell us how long it will last.

¹⁰ How long, O God, is the enemy to scoff?
>   Is the foe to insult your name forever?
¹¹ Why, O Lord, do you hold back your hand?
>   Why do you keep your right hand hidden in
>   your cloak?

¹² Yet God is my king from time past,
>   who bestows salvation through all the land.
¹³ It was you who divided the sea by your might,
>   who shattered the heads of the monsters in the sea.

¹⁴ It was you who crushed Leviathan's heads,
>   and gave him as food to the beasts of the desert.
¹⁵ It was you who opened up springs and torrents;
>   it was you who dried up ever-flowing rivers.

¹⁶ Yours is the day and yours is the night;
>   it was you who established the light and the sun.
¹⁷ It was you who fixed the bounds of the earth,
>   you who made both summer and winter.

¹⁸ Remember this, O LORD: the enemy scoffed!
　A senseless people insulted your name!
¹⁹ Do not give the soul of your dove to the beasts,
　nor forget the life of your poor ones forever.

²⁰ Look to the covenant; each cave in the land
　is a place where violence makes its home.
²¹ Do not let the oppressed be put to shame;
　let the poor and the needy bless your name.

²² Arise, O God, and defend your cause!
　Remember how the senseless revile you all the day.
²³ Do not forget the clamor of your foes,
　the unceasing uproar of those who defy you.

Psalm 75 (74)

¹ *For the Choirmaster. Intoned like "Do not destroy."*
　A Psalm of Asaph. A Song.

² We give praise to you, O God;
　we give praise, for your name is near.
　We recount your wonderful deeds.

3 "When I establish the appointed time,
  then I myself will judge with fairness.
4 Though the earth and all who dwell in it may
        rock,
  it is I who set firm its pillars.

5 To the boastful I say, 'Do not boast';
  to the wicked, 'Do not flaunt your strength,
6 do not flaunt your strength on high.
  Do not speak with insolent pride.'"

7 For neither from the east nor from the west,
  nor from the desert comes honor,
8 for God himself is the judge.
  One he humbles, another he exalts.

9 For the LORD holds a cup in his hand,
  full of wine, foaming and spiced.
  He pours it; they drain it to the dregs;
  all the wicked on the earth must drain it.

10 As for me, I will rejoice forever,
   and sing psalms to the God of Jacob.
11 I shall break the strength of the wicked,
   while the strength of the just will be exalted.

Psalm 76 (75)

1 *For the Choirmaster. With String Instruments.*
  A Psalm of Asaph. A Song.

2 God is renowned in Judah;
  in Israel his name is great.
3 His tent is set in Salem,
  and his dwelling place in Sion.
4 It was there he broke the flaming arrows,
  the shield, the sword, the armor.

5 Resplendent are you, more majestic
  than the everlasting mountains.
6 The stouthearted, despoiled, slept in death;
  none of the soldiers could lift a hand.
7 At your threat, O God of Jacob,
  horse and rider lay stunned.

8 You, you alone, strike terror.
   Who can stand in your presence,
      against the might of your wrath?

9 You uttered your sentence from the heavens;
   the earth in terror was still
10 when you arose, O God, to judge,
   to save all the humble of the earth.

11 For the rage of man only serves to praise you;
   you surround yourself with the survivors of wrath.
12 Make vows to the LORD your God and fulfill
         them.
   Let all around him pay tribute to the One who
         strikes terror,
13 who cuts short the breath of princes,
   who strikes terror in the kings of the earth.

Psalm 77 (76)

[1] *For the Choirmaster. Intoned like "Jeduthun."*
   Of Asaph. A Psalm.

[2] I cry aloud to God,
   cry aloud to God that he may hear me.

[3] In the day of my distress I seek the Lord.
   In the night my hands are raised unwearied;
   my soul refuses comfort.
[4] As I remember my God, I groan.
   I ponder, and my spirit faints.

[5] You keep my eyes from closing.
   I am troubled, unable to speak.
[6] I think of the days of long ago,
   and remember the years long past.
[7] At night I muse within my heart.
   I ponder, and my spirit questions.

[8] "Will the Lord reject us forever?
   Will he show us his favor no more?
[9] Has his mercy vanished forever?
   Has his promise come to an end?
[10] Has God forgotten his mercy,
   or in anger withdrawn his compassion?"

¹¹ I said, "This is what causes my grief:
    that the right hand of the Most High has changed."
¹² I remember the deeds of the LORD,
    I remember your wonders of old;
¹³ I muse on all your works,
    and ponder your mighty deeds.

¹⁴ Your way, O God, is in the holy place.
    What god is as great as our God?
¹⁵ You are the God who works wonders.
    Among the peoples you showed your power.
¹⁶ Your strong arm redeemed your people,
    the descendants of Jacob and Joseph.

¹⁷ The waters saw you, O God,
    the waters saw you and anguished.
    Yes, the depths were moved to tremble.
¹⁸ The clouds poured down with rain.
    The skies sent forth their voice;
    Your arrows flashed to and fro.

¹⁹ Your thunderous voice was in the whirlwind;
    your flashes lighted up the world.
    The earth was moved and trembled.
²⁰ Your way was through the sea,
    your path through the mighty waters,
    but the trace of your steps was not seen.

²¹ You guided your people like a flock
    by the hand of Moses and Aaron.

Psalm 78 (77)

¹ *A Maskil of Asaph.*

Give ear, my people, to my teaching;
incline your ear to the words of my mouth.
² I will open my mouth in a parable
and utter hidden lessons of the past.

³ The things we have heard and understood,
the things our fathers have told us,
⁴ these we will not hide from their children
but will tell them to the next generation:
the glories of the LORD and his might,
and the marvelous deeds he has done.

⁵ He established a decree in Jacob;
in Israel he set up a law.
To our fathers he gave a command
to make it known to their children,
⁶ that the next generation might know it,
the children yet to be born.

They should arise and declare it to their children,
⁷ that they should set their hope in God,
and never forget God's deeds,
but keep every one of his commands,

⁸ So that they might not be like their fathers,
   a defiant and rebellious generation,
   a generation whose heart was fickle,
   whose spirit was not faithful to God.

⁹ The sons of Ephraim, armed with the bow,
   turned back in the day of battle.
¹⁰ They failed to keep God's covenant,
   refused to walk according to his law.

¹¹ They forgot the things he had done,
   the wondrous works he had shown them.
¹² He did wonders in the sight of their fathers,
   in Egypt, in the plains of Zoan.

¹³ He divided the sea and led them through,
   and made the waters stand up like a wall.
¹⁴ By day he led them with a cloud;
   throughout the night, with a light of fire.

¹⁵ He split the rocks in the desert.
   He gave them plentiful drink, as from the deep.
¹⁶ He made streams flow out from the rock,
   and made waters run down like rivers.

¹⁷ Yet still they sinned against him,
   rebelled against the Most High in the desert.
¹⁸ In their heart they put God to the test
   by demanding the food they craved.

¹⁹ They spoke against God and said:
   "Can God spread a table in the wilderness?
²⁰ See, he struck the rock:
   water gushed forth and swept down in torrents.
   But can he also give us bread?
   Can he provide meat for his people?"

²¹ When he heard this, the LORD was angry.
   A fire was kindled against Jacob;
   his anger rose against Israel.
²² For they had no faith in God,
   and did not trust his saving power.

²³ Yet he commanded the clouds above,
   and opened the gates of heaven.
²⁴ He rained down manna to eat,
   and gave them bread from heaven.

²⁵ Man ate the bread of angels.
   He sent them abundance of food;
²⁶ the east wind he stirred up in the heavens,
   the south wind he directed by his might.

²⁷ He rained flesh upon them like dust,
   winged fowl like the sands of the sea.
²⁸ He let it fall in the midst of their camp,
   and all around their tents.

²⁹ So they ate and had their fill,
   what they craved, he gave them.

³⁰ But before they had sated their hunger,
   while the food was still in their mouths,
³¹ God's anger rose against them.
   He slew the strongest among them,
   struck down the flower of Israel.

³² Despite all this, they kept on sinning;
   they failed to believe in his wonders.
³³ So he ended their days like a breath,
   and their years in sudden terror.

³⁴ When he slew them, then they sought him,
   repented and earnestly sought God.
³⁵ They would remember that God was their rock,
   God the Most High their redeemer.

³⁶ Yet they deceived him with their mouths;
   they lied to him with their tongues.
³⁷ For their hearts were not steadfast toward him;
   they were not faithful to his covenant.

³⁸ Yet he who is full of compassion
   forgave them their sin and spared them.
   So often he held back his anger,
   and did not stir up all his rage.

³⁹ He remembered they were only flesh,
a breath that passes, never to return.
⁴⁰ They rebelled against him often in the desert,
and caused him pain in the wasteland!

⁴¹ Yet again they turned and tested God;
they provoked the Holy One of Israel.
⁴² They failed to remember his deeds
on the day he saved them from the foe,
⁴³ when he worked his signs in Egypt,
his wonders in the plains of Zoan.

⁴⁴ He turned their rivers into blood;
they could not drink from their streams.
⁴⁵ He sent swarms of insects to devour them,
and frogs to destroy them.
⁴⁶ He gave their crops to insects,
the fruit of their labor to the locust.

⁴⁷ He destroyed their vines with hail,
their sycamore trees with frost.
⁴⁸ He gave up their cattle to hail,
their herds to darts of lightning.

⁴⁹ He unleashed on them the heat of his anger,
fury, rage, and havoc,
a troop of destroying angels.

⁵⁰ He leveled a path for his anger.
   He did not spare their lives from death,
   but gave their livestock to the plague.
⁵¹ He struck all the firstborn in Egypt,
   the first vigor of youth from the dwellings of Ham.

⁵² Then he brought forth his people like sheep;
   like a flock he led them in the desert.
⁵³ He led them safely with nothing to fear,
   while the sea engulfed their foes.

⁵⁴ So he brought them to his holy land,
   to the mountain his right hand had won.
⁵⁵ He drove out the nations before them,
   and apportioned to each their heritage.
   The tribes of Israel he settled in their tents.

⁵⁶ With defiance they tested God Most High;
   they refused to obey his decrees.
⁵⁷ They strayed, faithless like their fathers;
   they betrayed him like a treacherous bow.
⁵⁸ They provoked God to wrath with their high
         places,
   made him jealous with the idols they served.

⁵⁹ God heard this and was filled with fury;
   he utterly rejected Israel.
⁶⁰ He forsook his dwelling place in Shiloh,
   the tent where he dwelt with man.

⁶¹ He gave his strength into captivity,
   his splendor to the hands of the foe.
⁶² He gave up his people to the sword,
   and showed his anger against his heritage.

⁶³ So fire devoured their young men,
   their maidens had no wedding songs;
⁶⁴ their priests fell by the sword,
   and their widows made no lament.

⁶⁵ Then the Lord awoke as if from sleep,
   like a warrior maddened by wine.
⁶⁶ He struck his foes from behind,
   and put them to shame forever.

⁶⁷ He rejected the tent of Joseph.
   He did not choose the tribe of Ephraim,
⁶⁸ but he chose the tribe of Judah,
   the mountain of Sion which he loves.
⁶⁹ He built his shrine like the heavens,
   or like the earth which he founded forever.

[70] And he chose his servant David,
and took him away from the sheepfolds.
[71] From the care of the ewes he brought him
to be shepherd of Jacob his people,
of Israel his own possession.

[72] He tended them with blameless heart;
with his skillful hands he led them.

Psalm 79 (78)

¹ *A Psalm of Asaph.*

O God, the nations have invaded your heritage;
they have profaned your holy temple.
They have made Jerusalem a heap of ruins.
² They have handed over the bodies of your
      servants
as food to feed the birds of heaven,
and the flesh of your faithful to the beasts of the
      earth.

³ They have poured out their blood like water
      round Jerusalem;
no one is left to bury the dead.
⁴ We have become the taunt of our neighbors,
the mockery and scorn of those around us.
⁵ How long, O Lᴏʀᴅ? Will you be angry forever?
Will your jealous anger burn like fire?

⁶ Pour out your rage on the nations,
those that do not know you,
kingdoms that do not call upon your name.
⁷ For they have devoured Jacob
and laid waste the place where he dwells.

8 Do not remember against us
   the guilt of former times.
   Let your compassion hasten to meet us;
   for we have been brought very low.

9 Help us, O God our savior,
   for the sake of the glory of your name.
   Free us and forgive us our sins,
   because of your name.

10 Why should the nations say, "Where is their
        God?"
    Before our eyes make it known among the
        nations
    that you avenge the blood of your servants that
        was shed!
11 Let the groans of the prisoners come before you,
    your strong arm reprieve those condemned to die.

12 Pay back to our neighbors seven times over
    the taunts with which they taunted you, O Lord.
13 Then we, your people, the flock of your pasture,
    will give you thanks forever and ever.
    From age to age we will recount your praise.

Psalm 80 *(79)*

¹ *For the Choirmaster. Intoned like "Lilies of*
Testimony." Of Asaph. A Psalm.

² O shepherd of Israel, hear us,
   you who lead Joseph like a flock:
   enthroned on the cherubim, shine forth
³ upon Ephraim, Benjamin, Manasseh.
   Rouse up your might and come to save us.

⁴ O God, bring us back;
   let your face shine on us, and we shall be saved.

⁵ How long, O Lᴏʀᴅ, God of hosts,
   will you be angry at the prayer of your people?
⁶ You have fed them with tears for their bread,
   an abundance of tears for their drink.
⁷ You have made us the taunt of our neighbors;
   our foes mock us among themselves.

⁸ O God of hosts, bring us back;
   let your face shine forth, and we shall be saved.

⁹ You brought a vine out of Egypt;
   you drove out the nations and planted it.
¹⁰ Before it you cleared the ground;
   it took root and filled the land.

¹¹ The mountains were covered with its shadow,
the cedars of God with its boughs.
¹² It stretched out its branches to the sea;
to the River it stretched out its shoots.

¹³ Then why have you broken down its walls?
It is plucked by all who pass by the way.
¹⁴ It is ravaged by the boar of the forest,
devoured by the beasts of the field.

¹⁵ God of hosts, turn again, we implore;
look down from heaven and see.

Visit this vine and protect it,
¹⁶ the vine your right hand has planted,
the son of man you have claimed for yourself.
¹⁷ They have burnt it with fire and cut it down.
May they perish at the frown of your face.

¹⁸ May your hand be on the man at your right
hand,
the son of man you have confirmed as your own.
¹⁹ And we shall never forsake you again;
give us life that we may call upon your name.

²⁰ O LORD God of hosts, bring us back;
let your face shine forth, and we shall be saved.

Psalm 81 (80)

¹ *For the Choirmaster. Upon* the gittith. *Of Asaph.*

² Sing joyfully to God our strength,
   shout in triumph to the God of Jacob.
³ Raise a song and sound the timbrel,
   the sweet-sounding harp and the lute;
⁴ blow the trumpet at the new moon,
   when the moon is full, on our feast.

⁵ For this is a statute in Israel,
   a command of the God of Jacob.
⁶ He made it a decree for Joseph,
   when he went out from the land of Egypt.

A voice I did not know said to me:
⁷ "I freed your shoulder from the burden;
   your hands were freed from the builder's basket.
⁸ You called in distress and I delivered you.

I answered, concealed in the thunder;
   at the waters of Meribah I tested you.
⁹ Listen, my people, as I warn you.
   O Israel, if only you would heed!

¹⁰ Let there be no strange god among you,
   nor shall you worship a foreign god.
¹¹ I am the LORD your God,
   who brought you up from the land of Egypt.
   Open wide your mouth, and I will fill it.

¹² But my people did not heed my voice,
   and Israel would not obey me.
¹³ So I left them in their stubbornness of heart,
   to follow their own designs.

¹⁴ O that my people would heed me,
   that Israel would walk in my ways!
¹⁵ At once I would subdue their foes,
   turn my hand against their enemies.

¹⁶ Those who hate the LORD would cringe before
        him,
   and their subjection would last forever.
¹⁷ But Israel I would feed with finest wheat,
   and satisfy with honey from the rock."

Psalm 82 (81)

¹ *A Psalm of Asaph.*

God stands in the divine assembly.
In the midst of the gods, he gives judgment.

² "How long will you judge unjustly,
and favor the cause of the wicked?
³ Do justice for the weak and the orphan;
give justice to the poor and afflicted.
⁴ Rescue the weak and the needy;
set them free from the hand of the wicked."

⁵ They neither know nor understand;
they walk about in darkness,
and all the earth's foundations are shaken.

⁶ I have said to you, "You are gods,
and all of you, sons of the Most High.
⁷ And yet, like men you shall die;
you shall fall, like any of the princes."

⁸ Arise, O God; judge the earth!
For all the nations are yours.

Psalm 83 (82)

¹ *A Song. A Psalm of Asaph.*

² O God, do not be silent;
  do not be still and unmoved, O God.
³ For your enemies raise a tumult;
  those who hate you lift up their heads.

⁴ They plot against your people,
  conspire against those you cherish.
⁵ They say, "Come, let us destroy them as a nation;
  let not the name of Israel be remembered."

⁶ They conspire with a single mind;
  against you they make a covenant:
⁷ the camps of Edom and of Ishmael,
  of Moab and Hagar,

⁸ Gebal and Ammon and Amalek,
  Philistia, with the people of Tyre.
⁹ Assyria, too, is their ally,
  and joins hands with the children of Lot.

¹⁰ Treat them like Midian, like Sisera,
  like Jabin at the River Kishon,
¹¹ those who were destroyed at Endor,
  whose bodies rotted on the ground.

¹² Make their captains like Oreb and Zeeb,
    all their princes like Zebah and Zalmunna,
¹³ the men who said, "Let us take
    the fields of God for ourselves."

¹⁴ My God, scatter them like the whirlwind,
    drive them like chaff in the wind!
¹⁵ As fire that burns away the forest,
    as the flame that sets the mountains ablaze,
¹⁶ drive them away with your tempest,
    and fill them with terror at your storm.

¹⁷ Cover their faces with shame,
    so that they seek your name, O LORD.
¹⁸ Shame and terror be theirs forever.
    Let them be disgraced; let them perish!

¹⁹ Let them know that you alone,
    you whose name is the LORD,
    are the Most High over all the earth.

Psalm 84 (83)

¹ *For the Choirmaster. Upon* the gittith. *Of the sons of Korah. A Psalm.*

² How lovely is your dwelling place,
   O LORD of hosts.
³ My soul is longing and yearning
   for the courts of the LORD.
   My heart and my flesh cry out
   to the living God.

⁴ Even the sparrow finds a home,
   and the swallow a nest for herself
   in which she sets her young, at your altars,
   O LORD of hosts, my king and my God.

⁵ Blessed are they who dwell in your house,
   forever singing your praise.
⁶ Blessed the people whose strength is in you,
   whose heart is set on pilgrim ways.

⁷ As they go through the Baca Valley,
   they make it a place of springs;
   the autumn rain covers it with pools.
⁸ They walk with ever-growing strength;
   the God of gods will appear in Sion.

⁹ O LORD God of hosts, hear my prayer;
   give ear, O God of Jacob.
¹⁰ Turn your eyes, O God, our shield;
   look on the face of your anointed.

¹¹ One day within your courts
   is better than a thousand elsewhere.
   The threshold of the house of God
   I prefer to the dwellings of the wicked.

¹² For the LORD God is a sun, a shield;
   the LORD will give us his favor and glory.
   He will not withhold any good
   to those who walk without blame.
¹³ O LORD of hosts, how blessed
   is the man who trusts in you!

Psalm 85 (84)

¹ *For the Choirmaster. Of the sons of Korah. A Psalm.*

² O LORD, you have favored your land,
  and brought back the captives of Jacob.
³ You forgave the guilt of your people,
  and covered all their sins.
⁴ You averted all your rage;
  you turned back the heat of your anger.

⁵ Bring us back, O God, our savior!
  Put an end to your grievance against us.
⁶ Will you be angry with us forever?
  Will your anger last from age to age?

⁷ Will you not restore again our life,
  that your people may rejoice in you?
⁸ Let us see, O LORD, your mercy,
  and grant us your salvation.

⁹ I will hear what the LORD God speaks;
  he speaks of peace for his people and his faithful,
  and those who turn their hearts to him.
¹⁰ His salvation is near for those who fear him,
  and his glory will dwell in our land.

¹¹ Merciful love and faithfulness have met;
  justice and peace have kissed.
¹² Faithfulness shall spring from the earth,
  and justice look down from heaven.

¹³ Also the LORD will bestow his bounty,
  and our earth shall yield its increase.
¹⁴ Justice will march before him,
  and guide his steps on the way.

Psalm 86 (85)

¹ *A Prayer of David.*

Turn your ear, O Lᴏʀᴅ, and answer me,
for I am poor and needy.
² Preserve my soul, for I am faithful;
save the servant who trusts in you, my God.

³ Have mercy on me, O Lord,
for I cry to you all the day long.
⁴ Gladden the soul of your servant,
for I lift up my soul to you, O Lord.

⁵ O Lord, you are good and forgiving,
full of mercy to all who call to you.
⁶ Give ear, O Lᴏʀᴅ, to my prayer,
and attend to my voice in supplication.

⁷ In the day of distress, I will call to you,
and surely you will answer me.
⁸ Among the gods there is none like you, O Lord,
nor works to compare with yours.

⁹ All the nations you have made shall come;
they will bow down before you, O Lord,
and glorify your name,
¹⁰ for you are great and do marvelous deeds,
you who alone are God.

¹¹ Teach me, O Lord, your way,
    so that I may walk in your truth,
    single-hearted to fear your name.

¹² I will praise you, Lord my God, with all my heart,
    and glorify your name forever.
¹³ Your mercy to me has been great;
    you have saved me from the depths of the grave.

¹⁴ The proud have risen against me, O God;
    a band of the ruthless seeks my life.
    To you they pay no heed.

¹⁵ But you, O God, are compassionate and
        gracious,
    slow to anger, O Lord,
    abundant in mercy and fidelity;
¹⁶ turn and take pity on me.

    O give your strength to your servant,
    and save the son of your handmaid.
¹⁷ Show me the sign of your favor,
    that my foes may see to their shame
    that you, O Lord, give me comfort and help.

Psalm 87 (86)

¹ *Of the sons of Korah. A Psalm. A Song.*

Founded by him on the holy mountain,
² the LORD loves the gates of Sion,
  more than all the dwellings of Jacob.
³ Of you are told glorious things,
  you, O city of God!

⁴ "Rahab and Babylon I will count
  among those who know me;
  of Tyre, Philistia, Ethiopia, it is told,
  'There was this one born.'
⁵ But of Sion it shall be said,
  'Each one was born in her.'"

He, the Most High, established it.
⁶ In his register of peoples the LORD writes,
  "Here was this one born."
⁷ The singers cry out in chorus,
  "In you, all find their home."

Psalm 88 (87)

1 *A Song. A Psalm. Of the sons of Korah. For the*
Choirmaster. Intoned like Mahalat Leannoth.
A Maskil. For Heman the Ezrahite.

2 O LORD and God of my salvation,
   I cry before you day and night.
3 Let my prayer come into your presence.
   Incline your ear to my cry.
4 For my soul is filled with evils;
   my life is on the brink of the grave.

5 I am reckoned as one in the tomb;
   I am like a warrior without strength,
6 like one roaming among the dead,
   like the slain lying in their graves,
   like those you remember no more,
   cut off, as they are, from your hand.

7 You have laid me in the depths of the pit,
   in regions that are dark and deep.
8 Your anger weighs down upon me;
   I am drowned beneath your waves.
9 You have taken away my friends;
   to them you have made me hateful.

Imprisoned, I cannot escape;
¹⁰ my eyes are sunken with grief.
I call to you, Lord, all day long;
to you I stretch out my hands.

¹¹ Will you work your wonders for the dead?
Will the shades rise up to praise you?
¹² Will your mercy be told in the grave,
or your faithfulness in the place of perdition?
¹³ Will your wonders be known in the dark,
your justice in the land of oblivion?

¹⁴ But I, O Lord, cry out to you;
in the morning my prayer comes before you.
¹⁵ Why do you reject me, O Lord?
Why do you hide your face from me?

¹⁶ I am wretched, close to death from my youth.
I have borne your trials; I am numb.
¹⁷ Your fury has swept down upon me;
your terrors have utterly destroyed me.

¹⁸ They surround me all the day like a flood;
together they close in against me.
¹⁹ Friend and neighbor you have taken away:
my one companion is darkness.

Psalm 89 (88)

¹ *A Maskil. For Ethan the Ezrahite.*

² I will sing forever of your mercies, O LORD;
through all ages my mouth will proclaim your
fidelity.
³ I have declared your mercy is established forever;
your fidelity stands firm as the heavens.

⁴ "With my chosen one I have made a covenant;
I have sworn to David my servant:
⁵ I will establish your descendants forever,
and set up your throne through all ages."

⁶ The heavens praise your wonders, O LORD,
your fidelity in the assembly of your holy ones.
⁷ For who in the skies can compare with the LORD,
or who is like the LORD among the heavenly
powers?
⁸ A God to be feared in the council of the holy
ones,
great and awesome to all around him.

⁹ O Lord God of hosts, who is your equal?
   You are mighty, O Lord, and fidelity surrounds
            you.
¹⁰ It is you who rule the raging of the sea;
   it is you who still the surging of its waves.
¹¹ It is you who crush Rahab underfoot like a
            corpse;
   you scatter your foes with your mighty arm.

¹² The heavens are yours, the earth is yours;
   you have founded the world and its fullness;
¹³ it is you who created the North and the South.
   Tabor and Hermon shout for joy at your name.

¹⁴ Yours is a mighty arm.
   Your hand is strong; your right hand is exalted.
¹⁵ Justice and right judgment are the pillars of your
            throne;
   merciful love and fidelity walk in your presence.

¹⁶ How blessed the people who know your praise,
   who walk, O Lord, in the light of your face,
¹⁷ who find their joy every day in your name,
   who make your justice their joyful acclaim.

¹⁸ For you are the glory of their strength;
   by your favor it is that our might is exalted.
¹⁹ Behold, the Lord is our shield;
   he is the Holy One of Israel, our king.

²⁰ Then you spoke in a vision.
   To your faithful ones you said,
   "I have set the crown on a warrior,
   I have exalted one chosen from the people.

²¹ I have found my servant David,
   and with my holy oil anointed him.
²² My hand shall always be with him,
   and my arm shall make him strong.

²³ The enemy shall never outwit him,
   nor shall the son of iniquity humble him.
²⁴ I will beat down his foes before him,
   and those who hate him I will strike.

²⁵ My mercy and my faithfulness shall be with him;
   by my name his might shall be exalted.
²⁶ I will stretch out his hand to the Sea,
   and his right hand upon the Rivers.

²⁷ He will call out to me, 'You are my father,
   my God, the rock of my salvation.'
²⁸ I for my part will make him my firstborn,
   the highest of the kings of the earth.

²⁹ I will keep my faithful love for him always;
   with him my covenant shall last.
³⁰ I will establish his descendants forever,
   and his throne as lasting as the days of heaven.

³¹ If his descendants forsake my law
  and refuse to walk as I decree,
³² and if ever they violate my statutes,
  failing to keep my commands:

³³ Then I will punish their offenses with the rod;
  then I will scourge them on account of their guilt.
³⁴ But I will never take back my mercy;
  my fidelity will never fail.
³⁵ I will never violate my covenant,
  nor go back on the promise of my lips.

³⁶ Once for all, I have sworn by my holiness.
  'I will never lie to David.
³⁷ His descendants shall continue forever.
  In my sight his throne is like the sun;
³⁸ like the moon, it shall endure forever,
  a faithful witness in the heavens.'"

³⁹ But yet you have spurned and rejected,
  you are angry with the one you have anointed.
⁴⁰ You have renounced your covenant with your
      servant,
  and dishonored his crown in the dust.

⁴¹ You have broken down all his walls,
  and reduced his fortresses to ruins.
⁴² All who pass by despoil him;
  he has become the taunt of his neighbors.

⁴³ You have exalted the right hand of his foes;
   you have made all his enemies rejoice.
⁴⁴ You have turned back the edge of his sword;
   you have not upheld him in battle.

⁴⁵ You have brought his glory to an end;
   you have hurled his throne to the ground.
⁴⁶ You have cut short the days of his youth;
   you have heaped disgrace upon him.

⁴⁷ How long, O LORD? Will you hide yourself
         forever?
   How long will your anger burn like a fire?
⁴⁸ Remember the shortness of my life,
   and how frail you have made the children of men.
⁴⁹ What man can live and never see death?
   Who can save himself from the grasp of the tomb?

⁵⁰ Where are your mercies of the past, O Lord,
   which you swore in your faithfulness to David?
⁵¹ Remember, O Lord, the taunts to your servant,
   how I have to bear all the insults of the peoples.
⁵² Thus your enemies lift up a taunt, O LORD,
   taunting your anointed at every step.

                *   *   *

[53] Blest be the LORD forever.
     Amen and amen!

BOOK FOUR
Of The Psalter

Psalm 90 *(89)*

¹ *Prayer of Moses, the man of God.*

O Lord, you have been our refuge,
from generation to generation.
² Before the mountains were born,
or the earth or the world were brought forth,
you are God, from age to age.

³ You turn man back to dust,
and say, "Return, O children of men."
⁴ To your eyes a thousand years
are like yesterday, come and gone,
or like a watch in the night.

⁵ You sweep them away like a dream,
like grass which is fresh in the morning.
⁶ In the morning it sprouts and is fresh;
by evening it withers and fades.

⁷ Indeed, we are consumed by your anger;
we are struck with terror at your fury.
⁸ You have set our guilt before you,
our secrets in the light of your face.

⁹ All our days pass away in your anger.
  Our years are consumed like a sigh.
¹⁰ Seventy years is the span of our days,
  or eighty if we are strong.
  And most of these are toil and pain.
  They pass swiftly and we are gone.

¹¹ Who understands the power of your anger?
  Your fury matches the fear of you.
¹² Then teach us to number our days,
  that we may gain wisdom of heart.

¹³ Turn back, O LORD! How long?
  Show pity to your servants.
¹⁴ At dawn, fill us with your merciful love;
  we shall exult and rejoice all our days.
¹⁵ Give us joy for the days of our affliction,
  for the years when we looked upon evil.

¹⁶ Let your deed be seen by your servants,
  and your glorious power by their children.
¹⁷ Let the favor of the Lord our God be upon us;
  give success to the work of our hands.
  O give success to the work of our hands.

Psalm 91 (90)

¹ He who dwells in the shelter of the Most High,
  and abides in the shade of the Almighty,
² says to the LORD, "My refuge,
  my stronghold, my God in whom I trust!"

³ He will free you from the snare of the fowler,
  from the destructive plague;
⁴ he will conceal you with his pinions,
  and under his wings you will find refuge.
  His faithfulness is buckler and shield.

⁵ You will not fear the terror of the night,
  nor the arrow that flies by day,
⁶ nor the plague that prowls in the darkness,
  nor the scourge that lays waste at noon.

⁷ A thousand may fall at your side,
  ten thousand fall at your right:
  you it will never approach.

⁸ Your eyes have only to look
  to see how the wicked are repaid.
⁹ For you, O LORD, are my refuge.
  You have made the Most High your dwelling.

¹⁰ Upon you no evil shall fall,
   no plague approach your tent.
¹¹ For you has he commanded his angels
   to keep you in all your ways.

¹² They shall bear you upon their hands,
   lest you strike your foot against a stone.
¹³ On the lion and the viper you will tread,
   and trample the young lion and the serpent.

¹⁴ Since he clings to me in love, I will free him,
   protect him, for he knows my name.
¹⁵ When he calls on me, I will answer him;
   I will be with him in distress;
   I will deliver him, and give him glory.

¹⁶ With length of days I will content him;
   I will show him my saving power.

Psalm 92 *(91)*

¹ *A Psalm. A Song for the Sabbath.*

² It is good to give thanks to the LORD,
  to make music to your name, O Most High,
³ to proclaim your loving mercy in the morning,
  and your truth in the watches of the night,
⁴ on the ten-stringed lyre and the lute,
  with the sound of song on the harp.

⁵ You have gladdened me, O LORD, by your deeds;
  for the work of your hands I shout with joy.
⁶ O LORD, how great are your works!
  How deep are your designs!
⁷ The senseless cannot know this,
  and the fool cannot understand.

⁸ Though the wicked spring up like grass,
  and all who do evil thrive,
  they are doomed to be eternally destroyed.
⁹ But you, O LORD, are eternally on high.

¹⁰ See, your enemies, O LORD,
  see, your enemies will perish;
  all who do evil will be scattered.

¹¹ To me you give the wild ox's strength;
  you have poured out on me purest oil.
¹² My eyes looked in triumph on my foes;
  my ears heard gladly of their fall.

¹³ The just will flourish like the palm tree,
   and grow like a Lebanon cedar.

¹⁴ Planted in the house of the LORD,
   they will flourish in the courts of our God,
¹⁵ still bearing fruit when they are old,
   still full of sap, still green,
¹⁶ to proclaim that the LORD is upright.
   In him, my rock, there is no wrong.

Psalm 93 (92)

¹ The LORD is king, with majesty enrobed.
  The LORD has robed himself with might;
  he has girded himself with power.

The world you made firm, not to be moved;
² your throne has stood firm from of old.
  From all eternity, O LORD, you are.

³ The floods have lifted up, O LORD,
  the floods have lifted up their voice;
  the floods have lifted up their thunder.

⁴ Greater than the roar of mighty waters,
  more glorious than the surgings of the sea,
  the LORD is glorious on high.

⁵ Truly your decrees are to be trusted.
  Holiness is fitting to your house,
  O LORD, until the end of time.

Psalm 94 *(93)*

¹ O Lord, avenging God,
   avenging God, shine forth!
² Judge of the earth, arise;
   give the proud what they deserve!

³ How long, O Lord, shall the wicked,
   how long shall the wicked triumph?
⁴ They bluster with arrogant speech;
   those who do evil boast to each other.

⁵ They crush your people, Lord;
   and they humble your inheritance.
⁶ They kill the widow and the stranger,
   and murder the fatherless child.

⁷ And they say, "The Lord does not see;
   the God of Jacob pays no heed."
⁸ Mark this, you senseless people;
   fools, when will you understand?

⁹ Can he who planted the ear not hear?
   Can he who formed the eye not see?
¹⁰ Will he who trains the nations not punish?
   Will he who teaches man not have knowledge?
¹¹ The Lord knows the plans of man.
   He knows they are no more than a breath.

¹² Blessed the man whom you discipline, O Lᴏʀᴅ,
   whom you train by means of your law;
¹³ to whom you give peace in evil days,
   while the pit is being dug for the wicked.

¹⁴ The Lᴏʀᴅ will not abandon his people,
   nor forsake those who are his heritage;
¹⁵ for judgment shall again be just,
   and all true hearts shall uphold it.

¹⁶ Who will stand up for me against the wicked?
   Who will defend me from those who do evil?
¹⁷ If the Lᴏʀᴅ were not to help me,
   my soul would soon go down to the silence.

¹⁸ When I think, "I have lost my foothold,"
   your mercy, O Lᴏʀᴅ, holds me up.
¹⁹ When cares increase in my heart,
   your consolation calms my soul.

²⁰ Can judges who do evil be your friends?
   They do injustice under cover of law;
²¹ they attack the life of the just,
   and condemn the innocent to death.

²² As for me, the Lᴏʀᴅ will be a stronghold;
   my God will be the rock where I take refuge.
²³ He will repay them for their wickedness,
   destroy them for their evil deeds.
   The Lᴏʀᴅ, our God, will destroy them.

Psalm 95 (94)

¹ Come, let us ring out our joy to the Lᴏʀᴅ;
  hail the rock who saves us.
² Let us come into his presence, giving thanks;
  let us hail him with a song of praise.

³ A mighty God is the Lᴏʀᴅ,
  a great king above all gods.
⁴ In his hands are the depths of the earth;
  the heights of the mountains are his.
⁵ To him belongs the sea, for he made it,
  and the dry land that he shaped by his hands.

⁶ O come; let us bow and bend low.
  Let us kneel before the God who made us,
⁷ for he is our God and we
  the people who belong to his pasture,
  the flock that is led by his hand.

O that today you would listen to his voice!
⁸ "Harden not your hearts as at Meribah,
    as on that day at Massah in the desert
⁹ when your forebears put me to the test;
    when they tried me, though they saw my work.

¹⁰ For forty years I wearied of that generation,
    and I said, 'Their hearts are astray;
    this people does not know my ways.'
¹¹ Then I took an oath in my anger,
    'Never shall they enter my rest.'"

Psalm 96 (95)

1 O sing a new song to the LORD;
  sing to the LORD, all the earth.
2 O sing to the LORD; bless his name.
  Proclaim his salvation day by day.
3 Tell among the nations his glory,
  and his wonders among all the peoples.

4 For the LORD is great and highly to be praised,
  to be feared above all gods.
5 For the gods of the nations are naught.
  It was the LORD who made the heavens.
6 In his presence are majesty and splendor,
  strength and honor in his holy place.

7 Give the LORD, you families of peoples,
  give the LORD glory and power;
8 give the LORD the glory of his name.

Bring an offering and enter his courts;
⁹ worship the LORD in holy splendor.
O tremble before him, all the earth.

¹⁰ Say to the nations, "The LORD is king."
The world he made firm in its place;
he will judge the peoples in fairness.

¹¹ Let the heavens rejoice and earth be glad;
let the sea and all within it thunder praise.
¹² Let the land and all it bears rejoice.

Then will all the trees of the wood shout for joy
¹³ at the presence of the LORD, for he comes,
he comes to judge the earth.
He will judge the world with justice;
he will govern the peoples with his truth.

Psalm 97 (96)

¹ The LORD is king, let earth rejoice;
  let the many islands be glad.
² Cloud and darkness surround him;
  justice and right are the foundation of his throne.

³ A fire prepares his path;
  it burns up his foes on every side.
⁴ His lightnings light up the world;
  the earth looks on and trembles.

⁵ The mountains melt like wax
  before the face of the LORD,
  before the face of the Lord of all the earth.
⁶ The skies proclaim his justice;
  all peoples see his glory.

⁷ Let those who serve idols be ashamed,
  those who boast of their worthless gods.
  All you angels, worship him.
⁸ Sion hears and is glad;
  the daughters of Judah rejoice
  because of your judgments, O LORD.

⁹ For you indeed are the LORD,
  most high above all the earth,
  exalted far above all gods.

¹⁰ The LORD loves those who hate evil;
   he guards the souls of his faithful;
   he sets them free from the wicked.

¹¹ Light shines forth for the just one,
   and joy for the upright of heart.
¹² Rejoice in the LORD, you just;
   to the memory of his holiness give thanks.

Psalm 98 (97)

¹ *A Psalm.*

O sing a new song to the LORD,
   for he has worked wonders.
His right hand and his holy arm
   have brought salvation.

² The LORD has made known his salvation,
   has shown his deliverance to the nations.
³ He has remembered his merciful love
   and his truth for the house of Israel.

All the ends of the earth have seen
   the salvation of our God.
⁴ Shout to the LORD, all the earth;
   break forth into joyous song,
   and sing out your praise.

5 Sing psalms to the LORD with the harp,
  with the harp and the sound of song.
6 With trumpets and the sound of the horn,
  raise a shout before the King, the LORD.

7 Let the sea and all within it thunder;
  the world, and those who dwell in it.
8 Let the rivers clap their hands,
  and the hills ring out their joy
9 at the presence of the LORD, for he comes,
  he comes to judge the earth.

He will judge the world with justice,
and the peoples with fairness.

Psalm 99 *(98)*

¹ The LORD is king; the peoples tremble.
   He is enthroned on the cherubim; earth quakes.
² The LORD is great in Sion.
   He is exalted over all the peoples.

³ Let them praise your great and awesome name.
   Holy is he!
⁴ O mighty King, lover of justice,
   you have established what is upright;
   you have made justice and right in Jacob.

⁵ Exalt the LORD our God;
   bow down before his footstool.
   Holy is he!

⁶ Among his priests were Aaron and Moses;
   among those who invoked his name was Samuel.
   They cried out to the LORD and he answered.

⁷ To them he spoke in the pillar of cloud.
   They obeyed his decrees and the statutes
   which he had given them.

⁸ O LORD our God, you answered them.
   For them you were a God who forgives,
   and yet you punished their offenses.

⁹ Exalt the LORD our God;
   bow down before his holy mountain,
   for the LORD our God is holy.

Psalm 100 (99)

¹ *A Psalm of Thanksgiving.*

Cry out with joy to the LORD, all the earth.
² Serve the LORD with gladness.
Come before him, singing for joy.

³ Know that he, the LORD, is God.
He made us; we belong to him.
We are his people, the sheep of his flock.

⁴ Enter his gates with thanksgiving
and his courts with songs of praise.
Give thanks to him, and bless his name.

⁵ Indeed, how good is the LORD,
eternal his merciful love.
He is faithful from age to age.

Psalm 101 (100)

¹ *Of David. A Psalm.*

I sing of merciful love and justice;
I raise a psalm to you, O LORD.
² I will ponder the way of the blameless.
O when will you come to me?

I will walk with blameless heart
within my house;
³ I will not set before my eyes
whatever is base.

I hate the deeds of the crooked;
I will have none of it.
⁴ The false-hearted must keep far away;
I will know no evil.

⁵ Whoever slanders a neighbor in secret
I will bring to silence.
Proud eyes and haughty heart
I will never endure.

⁶ My eyes are on the faithful of the land,
that they may dwell with me.
The one who walks in the way of the blameless
shall be my servant.

⁷ No one who practices deceit
shall live within my house.
One who utters lies
shall not stand before my eyes.

⁸ Morning by morning I will destroy
all the wicked in the land,
uprooting from the city of the LORD
all who do evil.

Psalm 102 (101)

¹ *Prayer of someone afflicted who is weary and pours*
out his trouble to the LORD.

² O LORD, hear my prayer,
and let my cry come to you.
³ Do not hide your face from me
in the day of my distress.

Turn your ear toward me;
on the day when I call,
speedily answer me.

⁴ For my days are vanishing like smoke;
my bones burn away like a furnace.
⁵ My heart is withered and dried up like the grass.
I forget to eat my bread.
⁶ Because of the sound of my groaning,
my skin clings to my bones.

⁷ I have become like a vulture in the desert,
like an owl among the ruins.
⁸ I lie awake and I moan,
like a bird alone on a roof.
⁹ All day long my foes revile me;
those who deride me use my name as a curse.

¹⁰ I have eaten ashes like bread,
    and mingled tears with my drink.
¹¹ Because of your anger and fury,
    you have lifted me up and thrown me down.
¹² My days are like a fading shadow,
    and I wither away like the grass.

¹³ But you, O Lord, are enthroned forever,
    and your renown is from age to age.

¹⁴ You will arise and take pity on Sion,
    for this is the time to have mercy;
    yes, the time appointed has come.
¹⁵ Behold, your servants love her very stones,
    are moved to pity for her dust.

¹⁶ The nations shall fear the name of the Lord,
    and all the earth's kings your glory.
¹⁷ When the Lord shall build up Sion,
    he will appear in all his glory.
¹⁸ Then he will turn to the prayers of the helpless;
    he will not despise their prayers.

¹⁹ Let this be written for ages to come,
    that a people yet unborn may praise the Lord;
²⁰ The Lord looked down from his holy place on
        high,
    looked down from heaven to the earth,
²¹ to hear the groans of the prisoners,
    and free those condemned to die.

²² May the name of the LORD be proclaimed in
      Sion,
  and his praise in Jerusalem,
²³ when peoples and kingdoms are gathered as one
  to offer their worship to the LORD.

²⁴ He has broken my strength in midcourse;
  he has shortened my days.
²⁵ I say: "My God, do not take me away
  before half of my days are complete,
  you, whose days last from age to age.

²⁶ Long ago you founded the earth,
  and the heavens are the work of your hands.
²⁷ They will perish but you will remain.
  They will all wear out like a garment.
  You will change them like clothes, and they
      change.
²⁸ But you are the same, and your years do not
      end."

²⁹ The children of your servants shall dwell
      untroubled,
  and their descendants established before you.

Psalm 103 (102)

¹ *Of David.*

Bless the LORD, O my soul,
   and all within me, his holy name.
² Bless the LORD, O my soul,
   and never forget all his benefits.

³ It is the Lord who forgives all your sins,
   who heals every one of your ills,
⁴ who redeems your life from the grave,
   who crowns you with mercy and compassion,
⁵ who fills your life with good things,
   renewing your youth like an eagle's.

⁶ The LORD does just deeds,
   gives full justice to all who are oppressed.
⁷ He made known his ways to Moses,
   and his deeds to the children of Israel.

⁸ The LORD is compassionate and gracious,
   slow to anger and rich in mercy.
⁹ He will not always find fault;
   nor persist in his anger forever.
¹⁰ He does not treat us according to our sins,
   nor repay us according to our faults.

¹¹ For as the heavens are high above the earth,
   so strong his mercy for those who fear him.
¹² As far as the east is from the west,
   so far from us does he remove our transgressions.

¹³ As a father has compassion on his children,
   the LORD's compassion is on those who fear him.
¹⁴ For he knows of what we are made;
   he remembers that we are dust.

¹⁵ Man, his days are like grass;
   he flowers like the flower of the field.
¹⁶ The wind blows, and it is no more,
   and its place never sees it again.

¹⁷ But the mercy of the LORD is everlasting
   upon those who hold him in fear,
   upon children's children his justice,
¹⁸ for those who keep his covenant,
   and remember to fulfill his commands.

¹⁹ The LORD has fixed his throne in heaven,
and his kingdom is ruling over all.
²⁰ Bless the LORD, all you his angels,
mighty in power, fulfilling his word,
who heed the voice of his word.

²¹ Bless the LORD, all his hosts,
his servants, who do his will.
²² Bless the LORD, all his works,
in every place where he rules.
Bless the LORD, O my soul!

Psalm 104 (103)

¹ Bless the LORD, O my soul!
  O LORD my God, how great you are,
  clothed in majesty and honor,
² wrapped in light as with a robe!

  You stretch out the heavens like a tent.
³ On the waters you establish your dwelling.
  You make the clouds your chariot;
  you ride on the wings of the wind.
⁴ You make the winds your messengers,
  flame and fire your servants.

⁵ You set the earth on its foundation,
  immovable from age to age.
⁶ You wrapped it with the depths like a cloak;
  the waters stood higher than the mountains.
⁷ At your threat they took to flight;
  at the voice of your thunder they fled.

⁸ The mountains rose, the valleys descended,
  to the place which you had appointed them.
⁹ You set limits they might not pass,
  lest they return to cover the earth.

¹⁰ You make springs gush forth in the valleys;
   they flow in between the hills.
¹¹ They give drink to all the beasts of the field;
   the wild asses quench their thirst.
¹² There the birds of heaven build their nests;
   from the branches they sing their song.

¹³ From your dwelling you water the hills;
   by your works the earth has its fill.

¹⁴ You make the grass grow for the cattle
   and plants to serve mankind's need.
   That he may bring forth bread from the earth
¹⁵ and wine to cheer the heart;
   oil, to make faces shine,
   and bread to strengthen the heart of man.

¹⁶ The trees of the LORD drink their fill,
   the cedars he planted on Lebanon;
¹⁷ there the birds build their nests;
   on the treetop the stork has her home.
¹⁸ For the goats the lofty mountains,
   for the rabbits the rocks are a refuge.

¹⁹ You made the moon to mark the months;
  the sun knows the time for its setting.
²⁰ You spread the darkness, it is night,
  and all the beasts of the forest creep forth.
²¹ The young lions roar for their prey,
  and seek their food from God.

²² At the rising of the sun they gather;
  and they go to lie down in their dens.
²³ Man goes forth to his work,
  to labor till evening falls.

²⁴ How many are your works, O LORD!
  In wisdom you have made them all.
  The earth is full of your creatures.

²⁵ Vast and wide is the span of the sea,
  with its creeping things past counting,
  living things great and small.
²⁶ The ships are moving there,
  and Leviathan you made to play with.

²⁷ All of these look to you
  to give them their food in due season.
²⁸ You give it, they gather it up;
  you open wide your hand, they are well filled.

²⁹ You hide your face, they are dismayed;
  you take away their breath, they die,
  returning to the dust from which they came.
³⁰ You send forth your spirit, and they are created,
  and you renew the face of the earth.

³¹ May the glory of the LORD last forever!
  May the LORD rejoice in his works!
³² He looks on the earth and it trembles;
  he touches the mountains and they smoke.

³³ I will sing to the LORD all my life,
  sing psalms to my God while I live.
³⁴ May my thoughts be pleasing to him.
  I will rejoice in the LORD.

³⁵ Let sinners vanish from the earth,
  and the wicked exist no more.
  Bless the LORD, O my soul.

  Alleluia!

Psalm 105 *(104)*

¹ Give thanks to the LORD; proclaim his name.
  Make known his deeds among the peoples.

² O sing to him, sing his praise;
  tell all his wonderful works!
³ Glory in his holy name;
  let the hearts that seek the LORD rejoice.

⁴ Turn to the LORD and his strength;
  constantly seek his face.
⁵ Remember the wonders he has done,
  his marvels and his words of judgment.

⁶ O children of Abraham, his servant,
  O descendants of the Jacob he chose,
⁷ he, the LORD, is our God;
  his judgments are in all the earth.

⁸ He remembers his covenant forever:
  the promise he ordained for a thousand
        generations,
⁹ the covenant he made with Abraham,
  the oath he swore to Isaac.

¹⁰ He confirmed it for Jacob as a law,
  for Israel as a covenant forever,
¹¹ saying, "I will give you the land of Canaan
  to be your allotted inheritance."

¹² When they were few in number,
a handful of strangers in the land,
¹³ when they wandered from nation to nation,
from one kingdom and people to another,

¹⁴ He allowed no one to oppress them;
he admonished kings on their account,
¹⁵ saying, "Those I have anointed, do not touch;
do no harm to any of my prophets."

¹⁶ But he called down a famine on the land;
he broke their staff of bread.
¹⁷ He had sent a man ahead of them,
Joseph, sold as a slave.

¹⁸ His feet were weighed down in chains,
his neck was bound with iron,
¹⁹ until what he said came to pass,
and the word of the LORD proved him true.

²⁰ Then the king sent orders and released him;
the ruler of the peoples set him free.
²¹ He made him master of his house
and ruler of all his possessions,
²² to instruct his princes from his heart,
and to teach his elders wisdom.

²³ So Israel came into Egypt;
    Jacob dwelt in the land of Ham.
²⁴ He gave his people great increase;
    he made them stronger than their foes,
²⁵ whose hearts he turned to hate his people,
    and to deal deceitfully with his servants.

²⁶ Then he sent Moses his servant,
    and Aaron whom he had chosen.
²⁷ They performed God's signs among them,
    and his wonders in the land of Ham.

²⁸ He sent darkness, and dark was made,
    but they rebelled against his words.
²⁹ He turned their waters into blood,
    and caused their fish to die.

³⁰ Their land was overrun by frogs,
    even to the halls of their kings.
³¹ He spoke; there came swarms of flies,
    and gnats covered all the country.

³² He sent hailstones in place of the rain,
    and lightning flashing in their land.
³³ He struck their vines and fig trees;
    he shattered the trees through their country.

³⁴ He spoke; the locusts came forth,
    young locusts, too many to be counted.
³⁵ They ate up every plant in the land;
    they ate up all the fruit of their fields.

³⁶ He struck all the firstborn in their land,
  the first fruit of all their strength.
³⁷ He led out Israel with silver and gold.
  In his tribes were none who stumbled.

³⁸ Egypt rejoiced when they left,
  for dread had fallen upon them.
³⁹ He spread a cloud as a screen,
  and fire to illumine the night.

⁴⁰ When they asked he sent them quails;
  he filled them with bread from heaven.
⁴¹ He pierced the rock and water gushed forth;
  it flowed as a river in the desert.

⁴² For he remembered his holy word,
  spoken to Abraham his servant.
⁴³ So he brought out his people with joy,
  his chosen ones with shouts of rejoicing.

⁴⁴ And he gave them the lands of the nations.
  Of other peoples they possessed the toil,
⁴⁵ that thus they might keep his precepts,
  that thus they might observe his laws.

Alleluia!

Psalm 106 (105)

¹ Alleluia!

O give thanks to the LORD, for he is good;
for his mercy endures forever.
² Who can tell the LORD's mighty deeds,
or recount in full his praise?

³ Blessed are they who observe what is just,
who at all times do what is right.
⁴ O LORD, remember me
with the favor you show to your people.

Visit me with your saving power,
⁵ that I may see the riches of your chosen ones,
and may rejoice in the gladness of your nation,
boasting in the glory of your heritage.

⁶ Like our fathers, we have sinned.
We have done wrong; our deeds have been evil.
⁷ Our forebears, when they were in Egypt,
did not grasp the meaning of your wonders.

They forgot the great number of your mercies,
at the Red Sea defied the Most High.
⁸ Yet he saved them for the sake of his name,
in order to make known his power.

9 He rebuked the Red Sea; it dried up,
   and he led them through the deep as through the
       desert.
10 He saved them from the hand of the foe;
   he freed them from the grip of the enemy.

11 The waters covered their oppressors;
   not one of them was left.
12 Then they believed in his words;
   then they sang his praises.

13 But they soon forgot his deeds,
   and would not wait upon his counsel.
14 They yielded to their cravings in the desert,
   and put God to the test in the wilderness.

15 He granted them the favor they asked,
   but struck them with a wasting disease.
16 In the camp, they were jealous of Moses,
   and also Aaron, who was holy to the LORD.

17 The earth opened and swallowed up Dathan,
   and buried the clan of Abiram.
18 Fire blazed up against their clan,
   and flames devoured the wicked.

19 They fashioned a calf at Horeb,
   and worshiped an image of metal;
20 they exchanged their glory
   for the image of a bull that eats grass.

²¹ They forgot the God who was their savior,
who had done such great things in Egypt,
²² such wonders in the land of Ham,
such marvels at the Red Sea.

²³ For this he said he would destroy them,
but Moses, the man he had chosen,
stood in the breach before him,
to turn back his anger from destruction.

²⁴ Then they scorned the desirable land;
they had no faith in his word.
²⁵ They complained inside their tents,
and did not listen to the voice of the LORD.

²⁶ So he raised his hand to them and swore
that he would lay them low in the desert,
²⁷ would disperse their descendants through the
nations
and scatter them throughout the lands.

²⁸ They bowed before the Baal of Peor,
ate offerings made to lifeless gods.
²⁹ They roused the LORD to anger with their deeds,
and a plague broke out among them.

³⁰ Then Phinehas stood up and intervened.
Thus the plague was ended,
³¹ and this was counted to him as righteous
from age to age forever.

³² They provoked him at the waters of Meribah.
   Through their fault it went ill with Moses,
³³ for they made his spirit grow bitter,
   and he uttered words that were rash.

³⁴ They failed to destroy the peoples,
   as the LORD had commanded them;
³⁵ instead they mingled with the nations,
   and learned to act as they did.

³⁶ They also served their idols,
   and these became a snare to entrap them.
³⁷ They even offered their sons
   and their daughters in sacrifice to demons.

³⁸ They poured out innocent blood,
   the blood of their sons and daughters,
   whom they offered to the idols of Canaan.
   The land was polluted with blood.

³⁹ So they defiled themselves by their actions;
   their deeds were those of a harlot.
⁴⁰ Then God's anger blazed against his people;
   he was filled with horror at his heritage.

⁴¹ So he handed them over to the nations,
   and their foes became their rulers.
⁴² Their enemies also oppressed them;
   they were subdued beneath their hand.

⁴³ Time after time he rescued them,
   but in their malice they dared to defy him
   and were weakened even more by their guilt.
⁴⁴ In spite of this he paid heed to their distress,
   so often as he heard their cry.

⁴⁵ For their sake he remembered his covenant.
   In the greatness of his mercy, he relented,
⁴⁶ and he let them be treated with compassion
   by all who held them captive.

⁴⁷ Save us, O LORD our God!
   And gather us from the nations,
   to give thanks to your holy name,
   and make it our glory to praise you.

*   *   *

[48] Blest be the LORD, God of Israel,
   forever, from age to age.
   Let all the people say,
   "Amen! Amen! Alleluia!"

BOOK FIVE
Of The Psalter

Psalm 107 (106)

1 "O give thanks to the LORD for he is good;
    for his mercy endures forever."
2 Let the redeemed of the LORD say this,
    those he redeemed from the hand of the foe,
3 and gathered from far-off lands,
    from east and west, north and south.

4 They wandered in a barren desert,
    finding no way to a city they could dwell in.
5 Hungry they were and thirsty;
    their soul was fainting within them.

6 Then they cried to the LORD in their need,
    and he rescued them from their distress,
7 and he guided them along a straight path,
    to reach a city they could dwell in.

8 Let them thank the LORD for his mercy,
    his wonders for the children of men;
9 for he satisfies the thirsty soul,
    and the hungry he fills with good things.

¹⁰ Some dwelt in darkness and the shadow of death,
  prisoners in misery and chains,
¹¹ having rebelled against the words of God,
  and spurned the plan of the Most High.
¹² He humbled their heart with toil.
  They stumbled; there was no one to help.

¹³ Then they cried to the LORD in their need,
  and he rescued them from their distress.
¹⁴ He led them out of darkness and the shadow of
      death,
  and broke their chains to pieces.

¹⁵ Let them thank the LORD for his mercy,
  his wonders for the children of men;
¹⁶ for he bursts the gates of bronze,
  and cuts through the iron bars.

¹⁷ Some fell sick on account of their sins,
  and were afflicted on account of their guilt.
¹⁸ They had a loathing for every food;
  they drew near to the gates of death.

¹⁹ Then they cried to the LORD in their need,
  and he rescued them from their distress.
²⁰ He sent forth his word to heal them,
  and saved their life from destruction.

²¹ Let them thank the LORD for his mercy,
   his wonders for the children of men.
²² Let them offer a sacrifice of thanks,
   and tell of his deeds with rejoicing.

²³ Some went down to the sea in ships,
   to trade on the mighty waters.
²⁴ These have seen the deeds of the LORD,
   the wonders he does in the deep.

²⁵ For he spoke and raised up the storm-wind,
   tossing high the waves of the sea
²⁶ that surged to heaven and dropped to the depths.
   Their souls melted away in their distress.

²⁷ They staggered and reeled like drunkards,
   for all their skill was gone.
²⁸ Then they cried to the LORD in their need,
   and he rescued them from their distress.

²⁹ He stilled the storm to a whisper,
   and the waves of the sea were hushed.
³⁰ They rejoiced because of the calm,
   and he led them to the haven they desired.

³¹ Let them thank the LORD for his mercy,
   his wonders for the children of men.
³² Let them exalt him in the assembly of the people,
   and praise him in the meeting of the elders.

³³ He changes rivers into desert,
   springs of water into thirsty ground,
³⁴ fruitful land into a salty waste,
   for the wickedness of those who live there.

³⁵ He changes desert into pools of water,
   thirsty ground into springs of water.
³⁶ There he settles the hungry,
   and they establish a city to dwell in.

³⁷ They sow fields and plant their vines,
   which yield an abundant harvest.
³⁸ He blesses them; they grow in numbers.
   He does not let their cattle decrease.

⁴⁰ He pours contempt upon princes,
   makes them wander in trackless wastes.
³⁹ They are diminished and brought low
   by oppression, evil, and sorrow.

⁴¹ But he raises the needy from distress;
   makes families numerous as a flock.
⁴² The upright see it and rejoice,
   while all the wicked close their mouths.

⁴³ Should not one who is wise recall these things,
   and understand the merciful deeds of the LORD?

Psalm 108 *(107)*

¹ *A Song. A Psalm of David.*

² My heart is ready, O God;
   my heart is ready.
   I will sing, I will sing your praise.
   Awake, my soul;
³ awake, O lyre and harp.
   I will awake the dawn.

⁴ I will praise you, LORD, among the peoples;
   I will sing psalms to you among the nations,
⁵ for your mercy reaches to the heavens,
   and your truth to the skies.

⁶ O God, be exalted above the heavens;
   may your glory shine on all the earth!
⁷ With your right hand, grant salvation and give
            answer;
   O come and deliver your friends.

⁸ From his holy place God has made this promise:
  "I will exult, and divide the land of Shechem;
  I will measure out the valley of Succoth.

⁹ Gilead is mine, as is Manasseh;
  Ephraim I take for my helmet,
  Judah is my scepter.
¹⁰ Moab is my washbowl;
  on Edom I will toss my shoe.
  Over Philistia I will shout in triumph."

¹¹ But who will lead me to the fortified city?
  Who will bring me to Edom?
¹² Have you not cast us off, O God?
  Will you march with our armies no longer?

¹³ Give us rescue against the foe,
  for human aid is vain.
¹⁴ With God, we shall do bravely,
  and he will trample down our foes.

Psalm 109 (108)

¹ *For the Choirmaster. Of David. A Psalm.*

O God whom I praise, do not be silent,
² for the mouths of deceit and wickedness
   are opened against me.

³ They speak to me with lying tongues;
   they beset me with words of hate,
   and attack me without cause.

⁴ In return for my love, they accuse me,
   while I am at prayer.
⁵ They repay me evil for good,
   hatred for love.

*　　*　　*

⁶ Appoint someone wicked over him;
   let an accuser stand at his right.
⁷ When he is judged, let him come out condemned;
   let his prayer be considered as sin.

⁸ Let the days of his life be few;
   let another assume his office.
⁹ Let his children be fatherless orphans,
   and his wife become a widow.

¹⁰ Let his children be wanderers and beggars,
    driven from the ruins of their home.
¹¹ Let the creditor seize all his goods;
    let strangers take the fruit of his work.

¹² Let no one show him any mercy,
  nor pity his fatherless children.
¹³ Let his posterity be destroyed,
  in a generation his name blotted out.

¹⁴ Let his father's guilt be remembered to the LORD,
  his mother's sin be retained.
¹⁵ Let it always stand before the LORD,
  that their memory be cut off from the earth.

¹⁶ For he did not think of showing mercy,
  but pursued the poor and the needy,
  hounding to death the brokenhearted.
¹⁷ He loved cursing; let curses fall on him.
  He scorned blessing; let blessing pass him by.

¹⁸ He put on cursing like his coat:
  let it sink into his body like water;
  let it sink like oil into his bones.
¹⁹ Let it be like the clothes that cover him,
  like a belt he wears all the time.

²⁰ Let the LORD thus repay my accusers,
  all those who speak evil against me.
²¹ But you, O LORD, my Lord,
  do with me as befits your name.
  How good your merciful love! Deliver me.

²² For I am poor and needy,
  and my heart is pierced within me.
²³ I fade like an evening shadow;
  I am shaken off like a locust.

²⁴ My knees are weak from fasting;
  my body is thin and gaunt.
²⁵ I have become an object of scorn;
  when they see me they shake their heads.

²⁶ Help me, LORD my God;
  save me with your merciful love.
²⁷ Let them know that this is your hand,
  that this is your doing, O LORD.

²⁸ They may curse, but you will bless.
  Let my attackers be put to shame,
  but let your servant rejoice.
²⁹ Let my accusers be clothed with dishonor,
  covered with shame as with a cloak.

³⁰ Loud thanks to the LORD are on my lips.
  I will praise him in the midst of the throng,
³¹ for he stands at the right hand of the poor,
  to save his soul from those who condemn him.

Psalm 110 (109)

¹ *Of David. A Psalm.*

The LORD's revelation to my lord:
"Sit at my right hand,
until I make your foes your footstool."

² The LORD will send from Sion
your scepter of power:
rule in the midst of your foes.

³ With you is princely rule
on the day of your power.
In holy splendor, from the womb before the dawn,
I have begotten you.

⁴ The LORD has sworn an oath he will not change:
"You are a priest forever,
in the line of Melchizedek."

⁵ The Lord, standing at your right,
shatters kings in the day of his wrath.

⁶ He brings a judgment among the nations,
and heaps the bodies high;
he shatters heads throughout the wide earth.

⁷ He shall drink from the stream by the wayside,
and therefore he shall lift up his head.

Psalm 110 (109)

¹ *Of David. A Psalm.*

Psalm 111 (110)

¹ Alleluia!

I will praise the LORD with all my heart,
  in the meeting of the just and the assembly.
² Great are the works of the LORD,
  to be pondered by all who delight in them.

³ Majestic and glorious his work;
  his justice stands firm forever.
⁴ He has given us a memorial of his wonders.
  The LORD is gracious and merciful.

⁵ He gives food to those who fear him;
  keeps his covenant ever in mind.
⁶ His mighty works he has shown to his people
  by giving them the heritage of nations.

⁷ His handiwork is justice and truth;
  his precepts are all of them sure,
⁸ standing firm forever and ever,
  wrought in uprightness and truth.

⁹ He has sent redemption to his people,
  and established his covenant forever.
  Holy his name, to be feared.

¹⁰ The fear of the LORD is the beginning of wisdom;
  understanding marks all who attain it.
  His praise endures forever!

Psalm 112 (111)

[1] Alleluia!

Blessed the man who fears the LORD,
who takes great delight in his commandments.
[2] His descendants shall be powerful on earth;
the generation of the upright will be blest.

[3] Riches and wealth are in his house;
his justice stands firm forever.
[4] A light rises in the darkness for the upright;
he is generous, merciful, and just.

[5] It goes well for the man who deals generously and
lends,
who conducts his affairs with justice.
[6] He will never be moved;
forever shall the just be remembered.

[7] He has no fear of evil news;
with a firm heart, he trusts in the LORD.
[8] With a steadfast heart he will not fear;
he will see the downfall of his foes.

[9] Openhanded, he gives to the poor;
his justice stands firm forever.
His might shall be exalted in glory.

[10] The wicked sees and is angry,
grinds his teeth and fades away;
the desire of the wicked leads to doom.

Psalm 113 (112)

[1] Alleluia!

Praise, O servants of the LORD,
praise the name of the LORD!
[2] May the name of the LORD be blest
both now and forevermore!
[3] From the rising of the sun to its setting,
praised be the name of the LORD!

[4] High above all nations is the LORD,
above the heavens his glory.
[5] Who is like the LORD, our God,
who dwells on high,
[6] who lowers himself to look down
upon heaven and earth?

[7] From the dust he lifts up the lowly,
from the ash heap he raises the poor,
[8] to set them in the company of princes,
yes, with the princes of his people.
[9] To the childless wife he gives a home
as a joyful mother of children.

Psalm 114 *(113A)*

¹ Alleluia!

When Israel came forth from Egypt,
the house of Jacob from a foreign people,
² Judah became his temple,
Israel became his domain.

³ The sea beheld them and fled;
the Jordan turned back on its course.
⁴ The mountains leapt like rams,
and the hills like yearling sheep.

⁵ Why was it, sea, that you fled;
that you turned back, Jordan, on your course?
⁶ O mountains, that you leapt like rams;
O hills, like yearling sheep?

⁷ Tremble, O earth, before the Lord,
in the presence of the God of Jacob,
⁸ who turns the rock into a pool,
and flint into a spring of water.

Psalm 115 *(113B)*

1 Not to us, O LORD, not to us,
   but to your name give the glory,
   for your merciful love and fidelity.
2 Why should the nations say:
   "Where is their God?"

3 But our God is in the heavens;
   he does whatever he wills.
4 Their idols are silver and gold,
   the work of human hands.

5 They have mouths but they cannot speak;
   they have eyes but they cannot see.
6 They have ears but they cannot hear;
   they have nostrils but they cannot smell.

7 They have hands but they cannot feel;
   they have feet but they cannot walk.
   They make no sound from their throats.
8 Their makers will come to be like them,
   as will all who trust in them.

⁹ House of Israel, trust in the LORD;
   he is their help and their shield.
¹⁰ House of Aaron, trust in the LORD;
   he is their help and their shield.
¹¹ Those who fear the LORD, trust in the LORD;
   he is their help and their shield.

¹² The LORD remembers us, and he will bless us;
   he will bless the house of Israel.
   He will bless the house of Aaron.

¹³ He will bless those who fear the LORD,
   the little no less than the great.
¹⁴ To you may the LORD grant increase,
   to you and all your children.

¹⁵ May you be blest by the LORD,
   the maker of heaven and earth.
¹⁶ The heavens, the heavens belong to the LORD,
   but to the children of men, he has given the earth.

¹⁷ The dead shall not praise the LORD,
   nor those who go down into the silence.
¹⁸ But we who live bless the LORD
   both now and forevermore.

   Alleluia!

Psalm 116A *(114:1–9; 115)*

¹ I love the LORD, for he has heard
 my voice, my appeal;
² for he has turned his ear to me
 whenever I call.

³ They surrounded me, the snares of death;
 the anguish of the grave has found me;
 anguish and sorrow I found.
⁴ I called on the name of the LORD:
 "Deliver my soul, O LORD!"

⁵ How gracious is the LORD, and just;
 our God has compassion.
⁶ The LORD protects the simple;
 I was brought low, and he saved me.

⁷ Turn back, my soul, to your rest,
 for the LORD has been good to you;
⁸ he has kept my soul from death,
 my eyes from tears, and my feet from stumbling.
⁹ I will walk in the presence of the LORD
 in the land of the living.

Psalm 116B *(115:10–19)*

¹⁰ I trusted, even when I said,
   "I am sorely afflicted,"
¹¹ and when I said in my alarm,
   "These people are all liars."

¹² How can I repay the LORD
   for all his goodness to me?
¹³ The cup of salvation I will raise;
   I will call on the name of the LORD.

¹⁴ My vows to the LORD I will fulfill
   before all his people.
¹⁵ How precious in the eyes of the LORD
   is the death of his faithful.

¹⁶ Your servant, LORD, your servant am I,
   the son of your handmaid;
   you have loosened my bonds.
¹⁷ A thanksgiving sacrifice I make;
   I will call on the name of the LORD.

¹⁸ My vows to the LORD I will fulfill
   before all his people,
¹⁹ in the courts of the house of the LORD,
   in your midst, O Jerusalem.

   Alleluia!

Psalm 117 (116)

¹ O praise the LORD, all you nations;
acclaim him, all you peoples!

² For his merciful love has prevailed over us;
and the LORD's faithfulness endures forever.

Alleluia!

Psalm 118 *(117)*

¹ Give praise to the LORD, for he is good;
  his mercy endures forever.

² Let the house of Israel say,
  "His mercy endures forever."
³ Let the house of Aaron say,
  "His mercy endures forever."
⁴ Let those who fear the LORD say,
  "His mercy endures forever."

⁵ I called to the LORD in my distress;
  he has answered and freed me.
⁶ The LORD is at my side; I do not fear.
  What can mankind do against me?
⁷ The Lord is at my side as my helper;
  I shall look in triumph on my foes.

⁸ It is better to take refuge in the LORD
  than to trust in man;
⁹ it is better to take refuge in the LORD
  than to trust in princes.

¹⁰ The nations all encircled me;
  in the name of the LORD I cut them off.
¹¹ They encircled me all around;
  in the name of the LORD I cut them off.

¹² They encircled me about like bees;
   they blazed like a fire among thorns.
   In the name of the LORD I cut them off.

¹³ I was thrust down, thrust down and falling,
   but the LORD was my helper.
¹⁴ The LORD is my strength and my song;
   he was my savior.

¹⁵ There are shouts of joy and salvation
   in the tents of the just.
   "The LORD's right hand has done mighty deeds;
¹⁶ his right hand is exalted.
   The LORD's right hand has done mighty deeds."

¹⁷ I shall not die, I shall live
   and recount the deeds of the LORD.
¹⁸ The LORD punished me, punished me severely,
   but did not hand me over to death.

¹⁹ Open to me the gates of justice:
   I will enter and thank the LORD.
²⁰ This is the LORD's own gate,
   where the just enter.
²¹ I will thank you, for you have answered,
   and you are my savior.

²² The stone that the builders rejected
   has become the cornerstone.
²³ By the Lord has this been done,
   a marvel in our eyes.
²⁴ This is the day the Lord has made;
   let us rejoice in it and be glad.

²⁵ O Lord, grant salvation;
   O Lord, grant success.
²⁶ Blest is he who comes
   in the name of the Lord.
   We bless you from the house of the Lord;
²⁷ the Lord is God, and has given us light.

   Go forward in procession with branches,
   as far as the horns of the altar.
²⁸ You are my God, I praise you.
   My God, I exalt you.
²⁹ Give praise to the Lord, for he is good;
   his mercy endures forever.

Psalm 119 (118):1–8
Aleph

¹ Blessed are those whose way is blameless,
  who walk in the law of the LORD!
² Blessed are those who keep his decrees!
  With all their hearts they seek him.

³ They never do anything evil,
  but walk in his ways.
⁴ You have laid down your precepts
  to be carefully kept.

⁵ May my ways be firm
  in keeping your statutes.
⁶ Then I shall not be put to shame
  as I observe all your commands.

⁷ I will thank you with an upright heart,
  as I learn your just judgments.
⁸ I will keep your statutes;
  do not ever forsake me.

Psalm 119 (118):9–16
Beth

9 How shall a youth remain pure on his way?
   By obeying your word.
10 I have sought you with all my heart;
   let me not stray from your commands.

11 I treasure your word in my heart,
   lest I sin against you.
12 Blest are you, O LORD;
   teach me your statutes.

13 With my lips have I recounted
   all the decrees of your mouth.
14 I rejoice in the way of your precepts,
   as though all riches were mine.

15 I will ponder your precepts,
   and consider your paths.
16 I take delight in your statutes;
   I will not forget your word.

Psalm 119 *(118):17–24*
Gimel

¹⁷ Deal bountifully with your servant,
    that I may live and keep your word.
¹⁸ Open my eyes, that I may see
    the wonders of your law.

¹⁹ I am a pilgrim in the land;
    hide not your commands from me.
²⁰ My soul is consumed with longing
    at all times for your decrees.

²¹ You threaten the proud, the accursed,
    who stray from your commands.
²² Free me from scorn and contempt,
    for I observe your decrees.

²³ Though princes sit plotting against me,
    your servant ponders your statutes.
²⁴ See, your decrees are my delight;
    your statutes are my counselors.

Psalm 119 (118):25–32
Daleth

[25] My soul holds fast to the dust;
   revive me by your word.
[26] I declared my ways and you answered me;
   teach me your statutes.

[27] Make me grasp the way of your precepts,
   and I will ponder your wonders.
[28] My soul pines away with grief;
   by your word raise me up.

[29] Keep me from the way of falsehood;
   grant me mercy by your law.
[30] I have chosen the way of faithfulness;
   your decrees I have upheld.

[31] I cling to your decrees, O LORD;
   let me not be put to shame.
[32] I will run the way of your commands;
   you open wide my heart.

Psalm 119 (118):33–40
He

33 LORD, teach me the way of your statutes,
   and I will keep them to the end.
34 Grant me insight that I may keep your law,
   and observe it wholeheartedly.

35 Guide me in the path of your commands,
   for in them is my delight.
36 Bend my heart to your decrees,
   and not to wrongful gain.

37 Turn my eyes from gazing on vanities;
   in your way, give me life.
38 Fulfill your promise to your servant,
   that you may be revered.

39 Turn away the taunts I dread,
   for your decrees are good.
40 See, I long for your precepts;
   give me life by your justice.

Psalm 119 (118):41–48
Vau

⁴¹ LORD, let your mercy come upon me,
the salvation you have promised.
⁴² I shall answer those who taunt me,
for I trust in your word.

⁴³ Never take the word of truth from my mouth,
for I hope in your decrees.
⁴⁴ I shall always keep your law,
forever and ever.

⁴⁵ I shall walk on a spacious plain,
for I seek your precepts.
⁴⁶ I will speak of your decrees before kings,
and not be abashed.

⁴⁷ In your commands I have found my delight;
these I have loved.
⁴⁸ I reach out to your commands, which I love,
and ponder your statutes.

Psalm 119 (118):49–56
Zayin

⁴⁹ Remember your word to your servant,
    by which you made me hope.
⁵⁰ This is my comfort in sorrow:
    that your promise gives me life.

⁵¹ Though the proud may utterly deride me,
    I do not turn from your law.
⁵² When I remember your judgments of old,
    these, O Lord, console me.

⁵³ I am seized with indignation at the wicked
    who forsake your law.
⁵⁴ Your statutes have become my song
    wherever I dwell.

⁵⁵ I remember your name in the nighttime,
    and I keep your law.
⁵⁶ This has been my lot,
    for I have kept your precepts.

Psalm 119 (118):57–64
Heth

[57] I have said, "O Lord, my portion
    is to obey your words."
[58] With all my heart I implore your favor;
    as with your promise, have mercy.

[59] I have pondered my ways,
    and turned my steps to your decrees.
[60] I made haste; I did not delay
    to obey your commands.

[61] Though the nets of the wicked ensnare me,
    your law I did not forget.
[62] At midnight I will rise and thank you
    for your just decrees.

[63] I am a friend of all who revere you,
    who keep your precepts.
[64] O Lord, your merciful love fills the earth.
    Teach me your statutes.

Psalm 119 (118):65–72
Teth

⁶⁵ O LORD, you have been good to your servant,
according to your word.
⁶⁶ Teach me good judgment and knowledge,
for I trust in your commands.

⁶⁷ Before I was humbled, I strayed,
but now I keep your word.
⁶⁸ You are good, and you do what is good;
teach me your statutes.

⁶⁹ The arrogant smear me with lies;
with all my heart I keep your precepts.
⁷⁰ Their heart is dense like fat,
but your law is my delight.

⁷¹ It was good for me to be humbled,
that I might learn your statutes.
⁷² The law from your mouth means more to me
than large quantities of silver and gold.

Psalm 119 (*118*):**73–80**
Yod

73 It was your hands that made me and shaped me;
   grant me insight to learn your commands.
74 Those who revere you see me and rejoice,
   for I trust in your word.

75 O LORD, I know that your decrees are right;
   though I am humbled, you are just.
76 Let your merciful love console me
   by your promise to your servant.

77 Show me compassion, that I may live,
   for your law is my delight.
78 Let the arrogant be shamed who deflect me with
        lies;
   as for me, I will ponder your precepts.

79 Let those who fear you turn to me,
   that they may know your decrees.
80 Let my heart be blameless in your statutes,
   that I may not be put to shame.

Psalm 119 (118):81–88
Caph

81 My soul yearns for your salvation;
   I hope in your word.
82 My eyes yearn to see your promise.
   I ask, "When will you comfort me?"

83 I am like a wineskin shriveled by smoke,
   yet I remember your statutes.
84 How long must your servant endure?
   When will you bring judgment on my foes?

85 For me the proud have dug pitfalls;
   they defy your law.
86 Your commands are all true; then help me
   when lies oppress me.

87 They have almost made an end of me on earth,
   yet I forsake not your precepts.
88 In your merciful love, give me life;
   I will obey the decrees of your lips.

Psalm 119 (118):89–96
Lamed

⁸⁹ Forever is your word, O LORD,
    standing firm in the heavens.
⁹⁰ From age to age is your truth;
    like the earth, it stands firm.

⁹¹ Your judgments endure to this day,
    for all things are your servants.
⁹² Had your law not been my delight,
    I would have died in my affliction.

⁹³ I will never forget your precepts,
    for with them you give me life.
⁹⁴ Save me, I am yours,
    for I seek your precepts.

⁹⁵ Though the wicked lie in wait to destroy me,
    yet I ponder your decrees.
⁹⁶ I have seen that all perfection has an end,
    but your command is boundless.

Psalm 119 (118):97–104
Mem

⁹⁷ O Lord, how I love your law:
  my meditation all the day!
⁹⁸ Your command makes me wiser than my foes,
  for it is with me always.

⁹⁹ I have more insight than all who teach me,
  for I ponder your decrees.
¹⁰⁰ I have gained more understanding than my
     elders,
  for I keep your precepts.

¹⁰¹ I keep my feet from every evil path,
  to obey your word.
¹⁰² I have not turned away from your decrees,
  which you yourself have taught me.

¹⁰³ How sweet is your promise to my tongue,
  more than honey in the mouth.
¹⁰⁴ I gain understanding from your precepts,
  and so I hate all false ways.

Psalm 119 (118):105–112
Nun

¹⁰⁵ Your word is a lamp for my feet,
 and a light for my path.
¹⁰⁶ I have sworn an oath and affirmed it,
 to obey your just judgments.

¹⁰⁷ I am deeply afflicted, O Lord;
 by your word, give me life.
¹⁰⁸ Accept, Lord, my freely offered homage,
 and teach me your decrees.

¹⁰⁹ My life is in my hands at all times;
 I do not forget your law.
¹¹⁰ For me the wicked have set a snare;
 yet I do not stray from your precepts.

¹¹¹ Your decrees are my heritage forever,
 the joy of my heart.
¹¹² I incline my heart to carry out your statutes
 forever, to the end.

Psalm 119 (118):113–120
Samech

[113] I detest those with a divided heart,
  but I love your law.
[114] You are my hiding place, my shield;
  I hope in your word.

[115] Depart from me, you who do evil;
  I will keep my God's commands.
[116] Uphold me by your promise; I shall live.
  Let my hopes not be in vain.

[117] Bear me up and I shall be saved,
  and ever muse on your statutes.
[118] You spurn all who stray from your statutes;
  their cunning is in vain.

[119] You regard the wicked like dross,
  so I love your decrees.
[120] My flesh trembles in terror before you;
  I fear your judgments.

Psalm 119 (118):121–128
Ayin

¹²¹ I have done what is just and right;
    do not leave me to my foes.
¹²² Guarantee the well-being of your servant;
    let not the proud oppress me.

¹²³ My eyes grow weary as I watch for your
        salvation,
    and for your promise of justice.
¹²⁴ Treat your servant with merciful love,
    and teach me your statutes.

¹²⁵ I am your servant; give me understanding:
    then I shall know your decrees.
¹²⁶ It is time for the LORD to act,
    for your law has been broken.

¹²⁷ That is why I love your commands
    more than finest gold,
¹²⁸ why I rule my life by your precepts,
    and hate false ways.

Psalm 119 (118):129–136
Pe

129 Your decrees are wonderful indeed;
    therefore my soul obeys them.
130 The unfolding of your word gives light,
    and understanding to the simple.

131 I have opened my mouth and I sigh,
    for I yearn for your commands.
132 Turn and have mercy on me,
    as is your rule for those who love your name.

133 Let my steps be guided by your promise;
    may evil never rule me.
134 Redeem me from man's oppression,
    and I will keep your precepts.

135 Let your face shine forth on your servant,
    and teach me your decrees.
136 My eyes shed streams of tears,
    because of those who have not kept your law.

Psalm 119 (118):137–144
Tsade

[137] You are just, O Lord;
   your judgments are upright.
[138] You have imposed your decrees with justice,
   and with utter fidelity.

[139] I am consumed with zeal,
   for my foes forget your word.
[140] Your promise has been thoroughly tested,
   and it is cherished by your servant.

[141] Although I am young and despised,
   I do not forget your precepts.
[142] Your justice is justice forever,
   and your law is truth.

[143] Though anguish and distress have found me,
   your commands are my delight.
[144] Your decrees are forever just;
   give me insight, and I shall live.

Psalm 119 (118):145–152
Koph

¹⁴⁵ I call with all my heart; LORD, answer me.
    I will observe your statutes.
¹⁴⁶ I call upon you; save me,
    and I will keep your decrees.

¹⁴⁷ I rise before dawn and cry for help;
    I have hoped in your word.
¹⁴⁸ My eyes awaken before dawn,
    to ponder your promise.

¹⁴⁹ In your mercy, hear my voice, O LORD;
    give me life by your decrees.
¹⁵⁰ Those who pursue me with malice draw near;
    they are far from your law.

¹⁵¹ But you, O LORD, are close;
    all your commands are truth.
¹⁵² From of old I have known that your decrees
    are established forever.

Psalm 119 (118):153–160
Resh

[153] See my affliction and deliver me,
    for I do not forget your law.
[154] Uphold my cause and defend me;
    by your promise, give me life.

[155] Salvation is far from the wicked,
    who are heedless of your statutes.
[156] Numberless, LORD, are your mercies;
    in your justice, give me life.

[157] Though my foes and oppressors are countless,
    I have not swerved from your decrees.
[158] I look at the faithless with disgust;
    they have not kept your word.

[159] See how I love your precepts, O LORD!
    In your mercy, give me life.
[160] Truth is the sum of your word;
    all your just judgments are eternal.

Psalm 119 (118):161–168
Shin

¹⁶¹ Though princes oppress me without cause,
my heart reveres your word.
¹⁶² I rejoice at your promise,
like one who finds a great treasure.

¹⁶³ Falsehood I hate and detest,
but I love your law.
¹⁶⁴ Seven times a day I praise you
for your just decrees.

¹⁶⁵ The lovers of your law have great peace;
no stumbling block for them.
¹⁶⁶ I await your salvation, O LORD;
I fulfill your commands.

¹⁶⁷ My soul obeys your decrees,
and loves them dearly.
¹⁶⁸ I obey your precepts and decrees;
all my ways are before you.

Psalm 119 (118):169–176
Tau

¹⁶⁹ Let my cry come before you, O LORD;
    give me insight by your word.
¹⁷⁰ Let my pleading come before you;
    rescue me according to your promise.

¹⁷¹ My lips shall proclaim your praise,
    because you teach me your statutes.
¹⁷² My tongue will sing of your promise,
    for your commands are just.

¹⁷³ Let your hand be ready to help me,
    for I have chosen your precepts.
¹⁷⁴ I have longed for your salvation, O LORD,
    and your law is my delight.

¹⁷⁵ My soul shall live and praise you.
    Your judgments give me help.
¹⁷⁶ I have strayed like a sheep; seek your servant,
    for I do not forget your commands.

Psalm 120 (119)

¹ *A Song of Ascents.*

To the LORD in the hour of my distress
I call—and he answers me.
² "O LORD, save my soul from lying lips,
from the tongue of the deceitful."

³ What should he give you, what repay you,
O deceitful tongue?
⁴ The warrior's arrows sharpened,
with red-hot coals from the broom tree!

⁵ Alas, that I live in Meshech,
dwell among the tents of Kedar!
⁶ I have had enough of dwelling
with those who hate peace.
⁷ I am for peace, but when I speak,
they are for war.

Psalm 121 (120)

¹ *A Song of Ascents.*

I lift up my eyes to the mountains;
from where shall come my help?
² My help shall come from the LORD,
who made heaven and earth.

³ He will keep your foot from stumbling.
Your guard will never slumber.
⁴ No, he sleeps not nor slumbers,
Israel's guard.

⁵ The LORD your guard, the LORD your shade
at your right hand.
⁶ By day the sun shall not smite you,
nor the moon in the night.

⁷ The LORD will guard you from evil;
he will guard your soul.
⁸ The LORD will guard your going and coming,
both now and forever.

Psalm 122 (121)

¹ *A Song of Ascents. Of David.*

I rejoiced when they said to me,
"Let us go to the house of the LORD."
² And now our feet are standing
within your gates, O Jerusalem.

³ Jerusalem is built as a city
bonded as one together.
⁴ It is there that the tribes go up,
the tribes of the LORD.

For Israel's witness it is
to praise the name of the LORD.
⁵ There were set the thrones for judgment,
the thrones of the house of David.

⁶ For the peace of Jerusalem pray,
"May they prosper, those who love you."
⁷ May peace abide in your walls,
and security be in your towers.

⁸ For the sake of my family and friends,
let me say, "Peace upon you."
⁹ For the sake of the house of the LORD, our God,
I will seek good things for you.

Psalm 123 *(122)*

¹ *A Song of Ascents.*

To you have I lifted up my eyes,
you who dwell in the heavens.

² Behold, like the eyes of slaves
on the hand of their lords,
like the eyes of a servant
on the hand of her mistress,
so our eyes are on the LORD our God,
till he show us his mercy.

³ Have mercy on us, LORD, have mercy.
We are filled with contempt.
⁴ Indeed, all too full is our soul
with the scorn of the arrogant,
the disdain of the proud.

Psalm 124 *(123)*

A Song of Ascents. Of David.

"If the LORD had not been on our side,"
let Israel say—
"If the LORD had not been on our side
when people rose against us,
then would they have swallowed us alive
when their anger was kindled.

Then would the waters have engulfed us,
the torrent gone over us;
over our head would have swept
the raging waters."

Blest be the LORD who did not give us
a prey to their teeth!
Our life, like a bird, has escaped
from the snare of the fowler.

Indeed, the snare has been broken,
and we have escaped.
Our help is in the name of the LORD,
who made heaven and earth.

Psalm 125 *(124)*

A Song of Ascents.

Those who put their trust in the LORD
are like Mount Sion, that cannot be shaken,
that stands forever.
Jerusalem! The mountains surround her;
so the LORD surrounds his people,
both now and forever.

For the scepter of the wicked shall not rest
over the land allotted to the just,
for fear that the hands of the just
should turn to evil.

Do good, LORD, to those who are good,
to the upright of heart;
but those who turn to crooked ways—
the LORD will drive away with the wicked!
On Israel, peace!

Psalm 126 (125)

¹ *A Song of Ascents.*

When the LᴀᴀD brought back the exiles of Sion,
we thought we were dreaming.
² Then was our mouth filled with laughter;
on our tongues, songs of joy.

Then the nations themselves said, "What great
deeds
the LᴀᴀD worked for them!"
³ What great deeds the LᴀᴀD worked for us!
Indeed, we were glad.

⁴ Bring back our exiles, O LᴀᴀD,
as streams in the south.
⁵ Those who are sowing in tears
will sing when they reap.

⁶ They go out, they go out, full of tears,
bearing seed for the sowing;
they come back, they come back with a song,
bearing their sheaves.

Psalm 127 (126)

¹ *A Song of Ascents. Of Solomon.*

If the LORD does not build the house,
in vain do its builders labor;
if the LORD does not guard the city,
in vain does the guard keep watch.

² In vain is your earlier rising,
your going later to rest,
you who toil for the bread you eat,
when he pours gifts on his beloved while they
slumber.

³ Yes, children are a gift from the LORD,
a blessing, the fruit of the womb.
⁴ Indeed, the sons of youth
are like arrows in the hand of a warrior.

⁵ Blessed is the warrior
who has filled his quiver with these arrows!
He will have no cause for shame,
when he disputes with his foes in the gateways.

Psalm 128 (127)

¹ *A Song of Ascents.*

Blessed are all who fear the LORD,
and walk in his ways!
² By the labor of your hands you shall eat.
You will be blessed and prosper.

³ Your wife like a fruitful vine
in the heart of your house;
your children like shoots of the olive
around your table.
⁴ Indeed thus shall be blessed
the man who fears the LORD.

⁵ May the LORD bless you from Sion.
May you see Jerusalem prosper
all the days of your life!
⁶ May you see your children's children.
On Israel, peace!

Psalm 129 (128)

¹ *A Song of Ascents.*

"They have pressed me hard from my youth,"
  let Israel sing.
² "They have pressed me hard from my youth,
  but could never overcome me.

³ The plowmen plowed my back,
  drawing long furrows.
⁴ Yet the LORD, who is just, has destroyed
  the yoke of the wicked."

⁵ Let them be shamed and routed,
  all those who hate Sion!
⁶ Let them be like grass on the roof,
  that withers before it flowers.

⁷ With that no reaper fills his hands,
  no binder of sheaves his arms.
⁸ And those passing by will not say,
  "The blessing of the LORD be upon you!"
  We bless you in the name of the LORD!

Psalm 130 (129)

¹ *A Song of Ascents.*

Out of the depths I cry to you, O LORD;
² Lord, hear my voice!
O let your ears be attentive
to the sound of my pleadings.

³ If you, O LORD, should mark iniquities,
Lord, who could stand?
⁴ But with you is found forgiveness,
that you may be revered.

⁵ I long for you, O LORD,
my soul longs for his word.
⁶ My soul hopes in the Lord
more than watchmen for daybreak.

More than watchmen for daybreak,
⁷ let Israel hope for the LORD.
For with the LORD there is mercy,
in him is plentiful redemption.
⁸ It is he who will redeem Israel
from all its iniquities.

Psalm 131 (130)

¹ *A Song of Ascents. Of David.*

O LORD, my heart is not proud,
nor haughty my eyes.
I have not gone after things too great,
nor marvels beyond me.

² Truly, I have set my soul
in tranquility and silence.
As a weaned child on its mother,
as a weaned child is my soul within me.

³ O Israel, wait for the LORD,
both now and forever.

Psalm 132 *(131)*

¹ *A Song of Ascents.*

O LORD, remember David
and all the hardships he endured,
² the oath he swore to the LORD,
his vow to the Strong One of Jacob.

³ "I will not enter my house,
nor go to the bed where I rest;
⁴ I will give no sleep to my eyes,
to my eyelids I will give no slumber,
⁵ till I find a place for the LORD,
a dwelling for the Strong One of Jacob."

⁶ At Ephrata we heard of it;
we found it in the plains of Yearim.
⁷ "Let us go to the place of his dwelling;
let us bow down at his footstool."

⁸ Go up, LORD, to the place of your rest,
you and the ark of your strength.
⁹ Your priests shall be clothed with justice;
your faithful shall ring out their joy.
¹⁰ For the sake of David your servant,
do not reject your anointed.

¹¹ The LORD swore an oath to David;
 he will not go back on his word:
 "A son, the fruit of your body,
 will I set upon your throne.

¹² If your sons hold fast to my covenant,
 and my laws that I have taught them,
 their sons, in turn, shall sit
 on your throne from age to age."

¹³ For the LORD has chosen Sion;
 he has desired it for his dwelling:
¹⁴ "This is my resting place from age to age;
 here have I chosen to dwell.

¹⁵ I will greatly bless her produce;
 I will fill her poor with bread.
¹⁶ I will clothe her priests with salvation,
 and her faithful shall ring out their joy.

¹⁷ I will make a stock sprout up for David;
 I will prepare a lamp for my anointed.
¹⁸ I will cover his enemies with shame,
 but on him my crown shall shine."

Psalm 133 (132)

¹ *A Song of Ascents. Of David.*

How good and how pleasant it is,
when brothers live in unity!

² It is like precious oil upon the head,
running down upon the beard,
running down upon Aaron's beard,
upon the collar of his robes;

³ Like the dew of Hermon, which runs down
on the mountains of Sion.
For there the LORD bestows his blessing:
life forever.

Psalm 134 (133)

[1] *A Song of Ascents.*

O come, bless the LORD,
all you servants of the LORD,
who stand by night in the courts
of the house of the LORD.
[2] Lift up your hands to the holy place,
and bless the LORD.

[3] May the LORD bless you from Sion,
he who made both heaven and earth.

Psalm 135 *(134)*

¹ Alleluia!

Praise the name of the LORD;
praise him, servants of the LORD,
² who stand in the house of the LORD,
in the courts of the house of our God.

³ Praise the LORD, for the LORD is good.
Sing a psalm to his name, for this is our delight.
⁴ For the LORD has chosen Jacob for himself,
and Israel as his treasured possession.

⁵ For I know that the LORD is great,
that our Lord is high above all gods.
⁶ The LORD does whatever he wills,
in heaven, and on earth,
in the seas, and in all the depths.

⁷ He summons clouds from the ends of the earth,
makes lightning produce the rain;
from his treasuries he sends forth the wind.

⁸ The firstborn of the Egyptians he smote,
of man and beast alike.
⁹ He sent signs and wonders in your midst, O
Egypt,
against Pharaoh and all his servants.
¹⁰ Nations in great numbers he struck,
and kings in their might he slew:

¹¹ Sihon, king of the Amorites,
  Og, the king of Bashan,
  and all the kingdoms of Canaan.
¹² Their land he gave as a heritage,
  a heritage to Israel, his people.

¹³ LORD, your name stands forever,
  your renown, LORD, from age to age.
¹⁴ For the LORD does justice for his people
  and takes pity on his servants.

¹⁵ Pagan idols are silver and gold,
  the work of human hands.
¹⁶ They have mouths but they do not speak;
  they have eyes but they do not see.

¹⁷ They have ears but they do not hear;
  there is never a breath on their lips.
¹⁸ Their makers will come to be like them,
  and so will all who trust in them!

¹⁹ House of Israel, bless the LORD!
  House of Aaron, bless the LORD!
²⁰ House of Levi, bless the LORD!
  You who fear the LORD, bless the LORD!
²¹ From Sion may the LORD be blest,
  he who dwells in Jerusalem!

  Alleluia!

Psalm 136 (135)

¹ O give thanks to the LORD, for he is good,
  for his mercy endures forever.
² Give thanks to the God of gods,
  for his mercy endures forever.
³ Give thanks to the Lord of lords,
  for his mercy endures forever;

⁴ Who alone has wrought marvelous works,
  for his mercy endures forever;
⁵ who in wisdom made the heavens,
  for his mercy endures forever;
⁶ who spread the earth on the waters,
  for his mercy endures forever.

⁷ It was he who made the great lights,
  for his mercy endures forever;
⁸ the sun to rule in the day,
  for his mercy endures forever;
⁹ the moon and the stars in the night,
  for his mercy endures forever.

¹⁰ The firstborn of the Egyptians he smote,
  for his mercy endures forever.
¹¹ He brought Israel out from their midst,
  for his mercy endures forever;
¹² with mighty hand and outstretched arm,
  for his mercy endures forever.

¹³ The Red Sea he divided in two,
for his mercy endures forever;
¹⁴ he made Israel pass through the midst,
for his mercy endures forever;
¹⁵ he flung Pharaoh and his force in the Red Sea,
for his mercy endures forever.

¹⁶ Through the desert his people he led,
for his mercy endures forever.
¹⁷ Nations in their greatness he struck,
for his mercy endures forever.
¹⁸ Kings in their splendor he slew,
for his mercy endures forever:

¹⁹ Sihon, king of the Amorites,
for his mercy endures forever;
²⁰ and Og, the king of Bashan,
for his mercy endures forever.

²¹ He gave their land as a heritage,
for his mercy endures forever;
²² a heritage for Israel, his servant,
for his mercy endures forever.
²³ He remembered us in our distress,
for his mercy endures forever.

²⁴ And he snatched us away from our foes,
for his mercy endures forever.
²⁵ He gives food to all living creatures,
for his mercy endures forever.
²⁶ To the God of heaven give thanks,
for his mercy endures forever.

Psalm 137 (136)

¹ By the rivers of Babylon
  there we sat and wept,
  remembering Sion;
² on the poplars that grew there
  we hung up our harps.

³ For it was there that they asked us,
  our captors, for songs,
  our oppressors, for joy.
  "Sing to us," they said,
  "one of Sion's songs."

⁴ O how could we sing
  the song of the LORD
  on foreign soil?
⁵ If I forget you, Jerusalem,
  let my right hand wither!

6 O let my tongue
 cleave to my palate
 if I remember you not,
 if I prize not Jerusalem
 as the first of my joys!

7 Remember, O LORD,
 against the children of Edom
 the day of Jerusalem,
 when they said, "Tear it down!
 Tear it down to its foundations!"

8 O daughter Babylon, destroyer,
 blessed whoever repays you
 the payment you paid to us!
9 Blessed whoever grasps and shatters
 your children on the rock!

Psalm 138 (137)

¹ *Of David.*

I thank you, Lord, with all my heart;
you have heard the words of my mouth.
In the presence of the angels I praise you.
² I bow down toward your holy temple.

I give thanks to your name
for your merciful love and your faithfulness.
You have exalted your name over all.
³ On the day I called, you answered me;
you increased the strength of my soul.

⁴ All earth's kings shall thank you, O Lord,
when they hear the words of your mouth.
⁵ They shall sing of the ways of the Lord,
"How great is the glory of the Lord!"

⁶ The Lord is high, yet he looks on the lowly,
and the haughty he knows from afar.
⁷ You give me life though I walk amid affliction;
you stretch out your hand against the anger of my
foes.

With your right hand you save me;
⁸ the Lord will accomplish this for me.
O Lord, your merciful love is eternal;
discard not the work of your hands.

Psalm 139 *(138)*

¹ *For the Choirmaster. Of David. A Psalm.*

O Lord, you search me and you know me.
² You yourself know my resting and my rising;
  you discern my thoughts from afar.
³ You mark when I walk or lie down;
  you know all my ways through and through.

⁴ Before ever a word is on my tongue,
  you know it, O Lord, through and through.
⁵ Behind and before, you besiege me,
  your hand ever laid upon me.
⁶ Too wonderful for me, this knowledge;
  too high, beyond my reach.

⁷ O where can I go from your spirit,
  or where can I flee from your face?
⁸ If I climb the heavens, you are there.
  If I lie in the grave, you are there.

⁹ If I take the wings of the dawn
  or dwell at the sea's furthest end,
¹⁰ even there your hand would lead me;
  your right hand would hold me fast.

¹¹ If I say, "Let the darkness hide me
and the light around me be night,"
¹² even darkness is not dark to you,
the night shall be as bright as day,
and darkness the same as the light.

¹³ For it was you who formed my inmost being,
knit me together in my mother's womb.
¹⁴ I thank you who wonderfully made me;
how wonderful are your works,
which my soul knows well!

¹⁵ My frame was not hidden from you,
when I was being fashioned in secret
and molded in the depths of the earth.

¹⁶ Your eyes saw me yet unformed;
and all days are recorded in your book,
formed before one of them came into being.

17 To me how precious your thoughts, O God;
  how great is the sum of them!
18 If I count them, they are more than the sand;
  at the end I am still at your side.

19 O God, that you would slay the wicked,
  that men of blood would depart from me!
20 With deceit they rebel against you,
  and set your designs at naught.

21 Do I not hate those who hate you,
  abhor those who rise against you?
22 I hate them with a perfect hate,
  and they are foes to me.

23 O search me, God, and know my heart.
  O test me, and know my thoughts.
24 See that my path is not wicked,
  and lead me in the way everlasting.

Psalm 140 *(139)*

¹ *For the Choirmaster. A Psalm of David.*

² Rescue me, LORD, from evil man;
   from the violent man keep me safe,
³ from those who plan evil in their hearts,
   and stir up strife every day;
⁴ who sharpen their tongue like an adder's,
   with the poison of viper on their lips.

⁵ LORD, guard me from the hands of the wicked;
   from the violent keep me safe;
   they plan to make me stumble.
⁶ The proud have hidden a trap,
   have spread out lines in a net,
   set snares across my path.

⁷ I have said to the LORD, "You are my God."
   Give ear, O LORD, to the cry of my appeal!
⁸ LORD, my Lord, my mighty help,
   you shield my head in the battle.
⁹ Do not grant, O LORD, the wicked their desire,
   nor let their plots succeed.

¹⁰ Those surrounding me lift up their heads.
   Let the malice of their speech overwhelm them.
¹¹ Let coals of fire rain upon them.
   Let them be flung in the abyss, no more to rise.
¹² Let the slanderer not endure upon the earth.
   Let evil quickly trap the violent!

¹³ I know the LORD will avenge the poor,
   that he will do justice for the needy.
¹⁴ Truly the just will give thanks to your name;
   the upright shall live in your presence.

Psalm 141 (140)

¹ *A Psalm of David.*

I have called to you, LORD; hasten to help me!
Hear my voice when I cry to you.
² Let my prayer be accepted as incense before you,
the raising of my hands like an evening oblation.

³ Set, O LORD, a guard on my mouth;
keep watch at the door of my lips!
⁴ Do not turn my heart to things that are evil,
to wicked deeds with those who are sinners.

Never allow me to share in their feasting.
⁵ If a good man strikes me it is kindness;
but let the oil of the wicked not anoint my head.
Let my prayer be ever against their malice.

⁶ If they fall into the merciless hands of their judges,
they will grasp how kind are my words.
⁷ As clods of earth plowed up on the ground,
so their bones were strewn at the mouth of the
grave.

⁸ To you my eyes are turned, O LORD, my Lord.
In you I take refuge; spare my soul!
⁹ From the trap they have laid for me, keep me safe;
keep me from the snares of those who do evil.

¹⁰ Let the wicked together fall into their traps,
while I pursue my way unharmed.

Psalm 142 (141)

¹ *A Maskil of David when he was in the cave.*
   A Prayer.

² With all my voice I cry to the LORD;
   with all my voice I entreat the LORD.
³ I pour out my trouble before him;
   I tell him all my distress
⁴ while my spirit faints within me.
   But you, O Lord, know my path.

   On the way where I shall walk,
   they have hidden a snare to entrap me.
⁵ Look on my right hand and see:
   there is no one who pays me heed.
   No escape remains open to me;
   no one cares for my soul.

⁶ To you I cry, O LORD.
   I have said, "You are my refuge,
   my portion in the land of the living."
⁷ Listen, then, to my cry,
   for I am brought down very low.

   Rescue me from those who pursue me,
   for they are stronger than I.
⁸ Bring my soul out of prison,
   and I shall give thanks to your name.
   Around me the just will assemble,
   because of your goodness to me.

Psalm 143 (142)

¹ *A Psalm of David.*

O Lord, listen to my prayer;
   turn your ear to my appeal.
   You are faithful, you are just; give answer.
² Do not call your servant to judgment,
   for in your sight no one living is justified.

³ The enemy pursues my soul;
   he has crushed my life to the ground.
   He has made me dwell in darkness,
   like the dead, long forgotten.
⁴ Therefore my spirit fails;
   my heart is desolate within me.

⁵ I remember the days that are past;
   I ponder all your works.
   I muse on what your hand has wrought,
⁶ and to you I stretch out my hands.
   Like a parched land my soul thirsts for you.

7 O LORD, make haste and answer me,
   for my spirit fails within me.
   Do not hide your face from me,
   lest I become like those
   who go down into the grave.

8 In the morning, let me know your loving mercy,
   for in you I place my trust.
   Make me know the way I should walk;
   to you I lift up my soul.

9 Rescue me, O LORD, from my foes;
   to you have I fled for refuge.
10 Teach me to do your will,
   for you are my God.
   Let your good spirit guide me
   upon ground that is level.

11 LORD, save my life for the sake of your name;
   in your justice, lead my soul out of distress.
12 In your mercy make an end of my foes;
   destroy all those who oppress my soul,
   for I am your servant.

Psalm 144 *(143)*

¹ *Of David.*

Blest be the LORD, my rock,
who trains my hands for battle,
who prepares my fingers for war.

² He is my merciful love, my fortress;
he is my stronghold, my savior,
my shield in whom I take refuge.
He brings peoples under my rule.

³ LORD, what is man that you regard him,
the son of man that you keep him in mind,
⁴ man who is merely a breath,
whose days are like a passing shadow?

⁵ Lower your heavens, O LORD, and come down.
Touch the mountains; wreathe them in smoke.
⁶ Flash your lightnings; rout the foe.
Shoot your arrows, and put them to flight.

⁷ Reach down with your hand from on high;
rescue me, save me from the mighty waters,
from the hands of foreign foes
⁸ whose mouths speak only emptiness,
whose hands are raised in perjury.

9 To you, O God, will I sing a new song;
   I will play on the ten-stringed harp
10 to you who give kings their victory,
   who set David your servant free
   from the evil sword.

11 Rescue me, free me from the hands of foreign
         foes,
   whose mouths speak only emptiness,
   whose right hands are raised in perjury.

12 Let our sons then flourish like saplings,
   grown tall and strong from their youth;
   our daughters graceful as columns,
   as though they were carved for a palace.

13 Let our barns be filled to overflowing
   with crops of every kind;
   our sheep increasing by thousands,
   tens of thousands in our fields,
14 our cattle heavy with young.

   No ruined wall, no exile,
   no sound of weeping in our streets.
15 Blessed the people of whom this is true;
   blessed the people whose God is the LORD!

Psalm 145 (144)

¹ *Praise. Of David.*

I will extol you, my God and king,
and bless your name forever and ever.

² I will bless you day after day,
and praise your name forever and ever.
³ The LORD is great and highly to be praised;
his greatness cannot be measured.

⁴ Age to age shall proclaim your works,
shall declare your mighty deeds.
⁵ They will tell of your great glory and splendor,
and recount your wonderful works.

⁶ They will speak of your awesome deeds,
recount your greatness and might.
⁷ They will recall your abundant goodness,
and sing of your just deeds with joy.

⁸ The LORD is kind and full of compassion,
slow to anger, abounding in mercy.
⁹ How good is the LORD to all,
compassionate to all his creatures.

¹⁰ All your works shall thank you, O LORD,
and all your faithful ones bless you.
¹¹ They shall speak of the glory of your reign,
and declare your mighty deeds,

¹² To make known your might to the children of
       men,
  and the glorious splendor of your reign.
¹³ Your kingdom is an everlasting kingdom;
  your rule endures for all generations.

  The LORD is faithful in all his words,
  and holy in all his deeds.
¹⁴ The LORD supports all who fall,
  and raises up all who are bowed down.

¹⁵ The eyes of all look to you,
  and you give them their food in due season.
¹⁶ You open your hand and satisfy
  the desire of every living thing.

¹⁷ The LORD is just in all his ways,
  and holy in all his deeds.
¹⁸ The LORD is close to all who call him,
  who call on him in truth.

¹⁹ He fulfills the desires of those who fear him;
  he hears their cry and he saves them.
²⁰ The LORD keeps watch over all who love him;
  the wicked he will utterly destroy.

²¹ Let my mouth speak the praise of the LORD;
  let all flesh bless his holy name
  forever, for ages unending.

Psalm 146 (145)

¹ Alleluia!

My soul, give praise to the LORD;
² I will praise the LORD all my life,
  sing praise to my God while I live.

³ Put no trust in princes,
  in mortal man who cannot save.
⁴ Take their breath, they return to the earth,
  and their plans that day come to nothing.

⁵ Blessed is he who is helped by Jacob's God,
  whose hope is in the LORD his God,
⁶ who made the heavens and the earth,
  the seas and all they contain,
  who preserves fidelity forever,
⁷ who does justice to those who are oppressed.

It is he who gives bread to the hungry,
  the LORD who sets prisoners free,
⁸ the LORD who opens the eyes of the blind,
  the LORD who raises up those who are bowed down.

It is the LORD who loves the just,
⁹ the LORD who protects the stranger
  and upholds the orphan and the widow,
  but thwarts the path of the wicked.
¹⁰ The LORD will reign forever,
  the God of Sion from age to age.

Alleluia!

Psalm 147A *(146:1–11)*

Alleluia!

1 How good to sing psalms to our God;
  how pleasant to chant fitting praise!

2 The LORD builds up Jerusalem
  and brings back Israel's exiles;
3 he heals the brokenhearted;
  he binds up all their wounds.
4 He counts out the number of the stars;
  he calls each one by its name.

5 Our Lord is great and almighty;
  his wisdom can never be measured.
6 The LORD lifts up the lowly;
  he casts down the wicked to the ground.
7 O sing to the LORD, giving thanks;
  sing psalms to our God with the harp.

8 He covers the heavens with clouds;
  he prepares the rain for the earth,
  making mountains sprout with grass,
  and plants to serve human needs.
9 He provides the cattle with their food,
  and young ravens that call upon him.

10 His delight is not in horses,
  nor his pleasure in a warrior's strength.
11 The LORD delights in those who revere him,
  those who wait for his merciful love.

Psalm 147B (147)

¹² O Jerusalem, glorify the LORD!
   O Sion, praise your God!
¹³ He has strengthened the bars of your gates;
   he has blessed your children within you.
¹⁴ He established peace on your borders;
   he gives you your fill of finest wheat.

¹⁵ He sends out his word to the earth,
   and swiftly runs his command.
¹⁶ He showers down snow like wool;
   he scatters hoarfrost like ashes.

¹⁷ He hurls down hailstones like crumbs;
   before such cold, who can stand?
¹⁸ He sends forth his word and it melts them;
   at the blowing of his breath the waters flow.

¹⁹ He reveals his word to Jacob;
   to Israel, his decrees and judgments.
²⁰ He has not dealt thus with other nations;
   he has not taught them his judgments.

Alleluia!

Psalm 148

¹ Alleluia!

Praise the LORD from the heavens;
   praise him in the heights.
² Praise him, all his angels;
   praise him, all his hosts.

³ Praise him, sun and moon;
   praise him, all shining stars.
⁴ Praise him, highest heavens,
   and the waters above the heavens.

⁵ Let them praise the name of the LORD.
   He commanded: they were created.
⁶ He established them forever and ever,
   gave a law which shall not pass away.

⁷ Praise the LORD from the earth,
   sea creatures and all ocean depths,
⁸ fire and hail, snow and mist,
   stormy winds that fulfill his command;

⁹ Mountains and all hills,
    fruit trees and all cedars,
¹⁰ beasts, both wild and tame,
    reptiles and birds on the wing;

¹¹ Kings of the earth and all peoples,
    princes and all judges of the earth,
¹² young men and maidens as well,
    the old and the young together.

¹³ Let them praise the name of the LORD,
    for his name alone is exalted,
    his splendor above heaven and earth.

¹⁴ He exalts the strength of his people.
    He is the praise of all his faithful,
    the praise of the children of Israel,
    of the people to whom he is close.

Alleluia!

Psalm 149

¹ Alleluia!

Sing a new song to the LORD,
his praise in the assembly of the faithful.
² Let Israel rejoice in its Maker;
let Sion's children exult in their king.
³ Let them praise his name with dancing,
and make music with timbrel and harp.

⁴ For the LORD takes delight in his people;
he crowns the poor with salvation.
⁵ Let the faithful exult in glory,
and rejoice as they take their rest.
⁶ Let the praise of God be in their mouths
and a two-edged sword in their hand,

⁷ To deal out vengeance to the nations
and punishment upon the peoples;
⁸ to bind their kings in chains
and their nobles in fetters of iron;
⁹ to carry out the judgment decreed.
This is an honor for all his faithful.

Alleluia!

Psalm 150

¹ Alleluia!

Praise God in his holy place;
  praise him in his mighty firmament.
² Praise him for his powerful deeds;
  praise him for his boundless grandeur.

³ O praise him with sound of trumpet;
  praise him with lute and harp.
⁴ Praise him with timbrel and dance;
  praise him with strings and pipes.

⁵ O praise him with resounding cymbals;
  praise him with clashing of cymbals.
⁶ Let everything that breathes praise the LORD!

Alleluia!